# STUDIES IN
# THE AGE OF GOETHE

# STUDIES IN
# THE AGE OF GOETHE

BY

MARSHALL MONTGOMERY
M.A., B.Litt.

READER IN GERMAN IN THE UNIVERSITY
OF OXFORD

OXFORD UNIVERSITY PRESS
LONDON: HUMPHREY MILFORD
1931

OXFORD UNIVERSITY PRESS
AMEN HOUSE, E.C. 4
LONDON EDINBURGH GLASGOW
LEIPZIG NEW YORK TORONTO
MELBOURNE CAPETOWN BOMBAY
CALCUTTA MADRAS SHANGHAI
HUMPHREY MILFORD
PUBLISHER TO THE
UNIVERSITY

PRINTED IN GREAT BRITAIN

# FOREWORD

THREE of the following studies (Nos. II, III, and V) have appeared in recent years in the Publications of the English Goethe Society. I am indebted to Professor J. G. Robertson, Litt.D., the editor of that organ, for kind permission to reprint these lectures, which have been carefully revised, but are substantially as there printed. Part of the fourth paper has appeared in the *Modern Language Review*, but it now includes some introductory pages, which are necessary to the proper development of the thesis put forward in the latter part of the article. The first study, that on 'Goethe's *Faust* as a Whole', has been written specially for this little work and has not appeared elsewhere.

While some of these papers have involved a certain amount of research, their main object is to offer other students of German literature some reflections on certain topics which are either too special to receive treatment in the current handbooks or are usually approached from a point of view which seems to me not to do them full justice. This is particularly the case in the essay on *Faust*, and it is my hope that even the members of the English Goethe Society may find in this study some not too familiar matter for consideration.

M. M.

OXFORD, 1930.

# CONTENTS

# I

## GOETHE'S *FAUST* AS A WHOLE

Ich fühlte gleich den Boden, wo ich stand; . . .
Und find' ich hier das Seltsamste beisammen,
Durchforsch' ich ernst dies Labyrinth der Flammen. (*Faust* II, 7075 ff.)

### 1. *The Disintegrating Critics*

Das sind die saubern Neuigkeiten,
Wo aus der Kehle, von den Saiten
Ein Ton sich um den andern flicht. (*Faust* II, 7172–4).

THE Middle Ages taught all Europe to think theologi-
cally. The Renaissance revived Greek studies, and by the
end of the eighteenth century it was once more fashionable
to think philosophically. Meanwhile the revival of natural
science combined with the beginnings of archaeology and
anthropology led to the search for origins and the study of evolution. In the nineteenth century the historian *pur sang* reigned
almost unchallenged, so that even philosophy and literature
were degraded to the level of the handmaidens of history.
Now, in the second quarter of the twentieth century, the conviction begins to grow upon us again that, without the philosophical spirit to inform it, all history is a desert of unmean-
ing facts and literature itself a collection of vain phantoms.
The true critic sees at last—more clearly than ever before—that
his success depends as much upon philosophical understanding
as upon historical inquiry. No work seems likely to gain more
from this new orientation than Goethe's masterpiece, *Faust*.

It has indeed always been known that a philosophical, or,
to speak more accurately, a theological, idea lies at the base
of Goethe's presentation of the Faust-legend. But misfortune
has lain in the gradual but steady trend of scholarship away
from this elementary truth and towards the analysis of the
evolution of the legend, which at one time almost bade fair
to throw the poem itself into obscurity. Just as for the
anthropologist *pithecanthropus* became a more fascinating
figure than Dante or Shakespeare, so in the mind of the

philologist the *Volksbuch*, the Puppenspiel, and finally the 'excavation' of the *Urfaust* became more absorbing topics than the finished work of the great poet. These things lent themselves readily to the historical analysis so beloved of the research-worker; the finished work was for him but the last and, to tell the truth, the least interesting stage in the evolution of the legend. And since it was 'made up' of so many elements which could be shown to exist by themselves in an earlier, more naked form, it lacked the charm of the primitive and was considered *ex hypothesi* deficient in spontaneity and overweighted with complex and heterogeneous materials. Moreover it had been—witness the *Urfaust*—nearly sixty years a-making. It was not a work 'aus einem Guss'. It might be compared to a great cathedral, perhaps; only it was doubtful whether it ever had a 'Grundplan', or alternatively, as the lawyers say, the 'Grundplan' had apparently been abandoned by the architect-builder before the structure was half complete. How, men said, could Goethe, the young Titan, and Goethe, the aged Olympian, have worked to the same plan? The thing, on the face of it, looked somewhat ridiculous. The historian, supported by 'facts', knew better than that. We need not be too severe upon men like C. H. Weisse, Vischer, and Vilmar for propagating the theory of the two *Fausts* or suggesting that the Second Part was 'nearly without meaning or interest'. Goethe himself was in part to blame with his talk of what he had 'hineingeheimnisst'. In England probably more weight still has been attached to the inadequate but solemnly given verdict of August Wilhelm Schlegel [1] on the first part, in which he says of Goethe:

> To the youthful epoch belongs his *Faust*, a work which was early planned, though not published till a late period, and which

[1] *Lectures on Dramatic Art and Literature* (originally translated by John Black); cited from the revised version by A. J. W. Morrison, published in 'Bohn's Standard Library' in 1879, p. 517.

even in its latest shape is still a fragment, and from its very nature perhaps must always remain so. It is hard to say whether we are here more lost in astonishment at the heights which the poet frequently reaches, or seized with giddiness at the depths which he lays open to our sight. But this is not the place to express the whole of our admiration of this labyrinthine and boundless work, the peculiar creation of Goethe: we have merely to consider it in a dramatic point of view. . . . Goethe's work, which in some points adheres closely to the tradition, but leaves it entirely in others, purposely runs out in all directions beyond the dimensions of the theatre. . . .

There is much more here, but all to the same effect, and what Schlegel had said in criticism of Part I was only too readily considered to apply to Part II and to the work as a whole. The adverse views of Coleridge and Lamb are too well known to be cited; even G. H. Lewes, in his almost passionate defence of Goethe's *Faust*, warns us not to expect too much from the Second Part, and when he comes to discuss it in his penultimate chapter confesses himself among those of 'Goethe's most loving students' who find it to be 'of mediocre interest, very far inferior to the *First Part*, and both in conception and execution an elaborate mistake'.

It would not be worth while to cite again such familiar critical opinions, if the views they put forward were mere aberrations of a dead and buried past. Unhappily there is only too much evidence to prove that even now, nearly a century after Goethe's death, there are many critics and thousands of readers who, more or less consciously, still grope blindly after the key to the unity of this great work, or more idly content themselves with recognizing the beauty of particular fragments—*disjecta membra*, they imagine, of an exploded whole. The strictures of the *Quarterly Review* (1834), the *Dublin Review* (1840), and Lewes himself (1855) have probably been echoed more often by English writers than the panegyrics of Carlyle and Blackie. The latter, M. Carré assures us,[1] was the first British critic to become aware that *Faust* is 'une œuvre d'art, et non une œuvre de prédication'. But 'la critique' as a whole 'ne montre pas une grande pénétration' either before or after 1850, so far as the study of *Faust* as a whole is concerned. From Matthew Arnold himself down to his latest critic[2] we discern with difficulty any clear appreciation of the real unity of idea underlying, supporting, and binding together the two parts, so soon, at least, as we pass beyond the most general remarks. Here and there, of course, exceptions exist to prove that we are not a wholly uncritical people. The influence of J. S. Blackie and of the earlier German 'unitarians', little read as they have been in this country, has not passed quite unnoticed, but in general the impression made upon the reading public is parallel to that left upon Goethe's biographer Hayward, who introduces his chapter on *Faust* with the remark, 'In what follows, "Faust" must be understood as the First Part unless the Second is specified.' His later references to this part are too unfortunate to be worth citing. One had hoped, too optimistically, that the influence of M. Edmond Scherer, to whom these English critics owe so much, had evaporated for ever, but one or two recent discussions point all too clearly to the inheritance of these strangely inadequate theories by certain writers of our own day.[3] To attempt to refute these criticisms *seriatim* is beyond the purpose of this essay. It seems wiser to approach the subject from the opposite angle by stating, however briefly, the case for those who persist in regarding *Faust*—the whole *Faust*—as a unified work of art.

[1] *Goethe en Angleterre*, deuxième éd., Paris 1920, pp. 229–31.
[2] J. B. Orrick, *Matthew Arnold and Goethe* (Publ. of the English Goethe Society, N.S., vol. iv, London, 1928).
[3] See especially the anonymous article on *Goethe's Faust* published in *The Times Literary Supplement* for Thursday, December 13, 1928. Even Professor J. G. Robertson in his recent *Life of Goethe* (London, 1927) has committed himself to the most extreme view of Goethe's 'degeneration' (as an artist) after 1788. He goes so far as to write (at p. 137), 'he who believed that he had "found himself" in Italy as an artist, had in reality lost there his artist's soul.'

Fortunately one's hands have been recently strengthened
by some very able German studies, which as yet seem to be
almost unknown in this country.[1]

'L'art de Goethe est ce qui est le plus difficile à faire com-
prendre en Angleterre.'[2] M. Jean-Marie Carré is justified by
our experience. Let us not inquire too closely how much of
this difficulty is due to our French mentors and how much to
the Germans themselves. Many of the latter, in this respect,
have set us an example we have found only too easy to imitate.
The 'Gehalt' of *Faust* is so noteworthy that the philosophic,
but too often unaesthetic, German mind has been thereby
misled into disregarding or belittling the 'Gestalt'. Herr
Julius Bab, for example, has recently written a valuable study
entitled *Faust, das Werk des Goetheschen Lebens*,[3] but in his
introduction he is at the greatest pains to explain—of course,
with the aid of Goethe's own verses—that 'es sich hier nicht
um ein Kunstwerk handelt, das nach klarem Plan einen
Anfang und ein Ende erhalten hat'. And he continues to
harp upon this string: 'in der Tat, dieses Gedicht gleicht,
von seinem Gehalt ganz abgesehen, als Form, als Geschöpf
dem Leben, weil es nicht im üblichen Sinne das Werk eines
Menschen ist, kein geschaffenes Werk, sondern ein gewordenes, ein gewachsenes! Und deshalb ohne die unnatürlich-
übernatürliche helle Umgrenzung der Kunst, vielmehr
dunkel verschwimmend in Geburt und Tod wie alles
Lebendige.' As if every true work of art were not *ein
gewachsenes und gewordenes*! Alas, why did not Horace write
one more *bon mot*, which every critic might have posted above
his desk—*poema nascitur, atque fit*!

It is incontrovertible—*Faust* grew! I have elsewhere compared it to a mighty and somewhat gnarled and weather-

---

[1] The essays of Burdach, Rickert, and Gerland are the most valuable.
[2] J.-M. Carré, *Goethe en Angleterre*, deuxième éd. (Paris, 1920), p. 294, following
the passage on 'le défaut de la critique de Matthew Arnold: il n'a pas le sens
artistique. . . . Il ressemble sur ce point à Carlyle.'
[3] Second ed., Stuttgart, &c., 1926.

beaten tree. But the simile, like all similes, is intended only
to express a portion of the truth. It is true that it grew; it
is no less true that it was made. It was born of the spirit,
but conceived in mental activity and brought forth with the
pains of labour. Goethe might well have parodied himself
and given it the motto:

> Nur wer die Sorge kennt,
> Weiss was ich leiste!

Truly this kind of work goeth not forth, save with prayer and
fasting. Equally it does not reveal its form, any more than
its meaning, to the first glance of an idle eye. This form is
not a circle or a square, but an intricate, highly-wrought
pattern. The mere relation of what is contained in the poem,
however skilfully achieved, gives a completely inadequate
impression of the whole. 'Denn der Gehalt der Dichtung
wird nur zum Teil begrifflich ausgesprochen, überdies nur
nach seiner minder wichtigen Seite. Das Eigentliche und
Letzte zu künden, bleibt der künstlerischen Gestalt der Dichtung überlassen'.[1] The 'Gehalt' and the 'Gestalt' are in fact,
as in every true work of art, only separable by a process of
abstraction which resembles the dissolution of body and soul.
Yet, for the same reason, the study of the 'Gehalt' helps
towards the understanding of the 'Gestalt', and vice versa.

'Aesthetics', says a humorous writer of to-day,[2] 'generally
lead to blows from lack of fixed standards, and the best
solution will probably be a strict adherence to the standards
of antiquity.' Both Goethe and Schiller were profoundly
impressed with the value of the standards of antiquity for
aesthetic judgements, though neither of them thought it
necessary to adhere rigidly to these standards. It is clear to
anyone who is willing to abandon, for a while at least, the
purely historical or genetic method of study and to look at

---

[1] Oskar Walzel, *Vom Wesen der Dichtung* (Leipzig, 1928), p. 15.
[2] *The Times* fourth leader, April 6, 1929, apropos of 'an Anti-Ugliness League'
newly formed in Germany.

*Faust* as a whole—as if, let us say, it had appeared as a single work in 1833—that classical standards are not therein closely followed. It should be equally clear that the work is far from being uninfluenced by the classical root-ideas of balance, harmony, and grandeur. But Erwin von Steinbach and Dante, Shakespeare and the baroque have come between ; Rousseau, too, and the Romantics have passed this way. And over all broods the Germanic spirit, ever ready in the midst of time to cast a longing gaze upon eternity. The complexity of the elements of this work is undeniable, yet this complexity yields to analysis, revealing beneath the richly decorated surface the simpler outlines of the supporting structure.

There is a common theory, much encouraged by our modern deference to the charms of youth and inexperience, that the best poetry and art have nearly all been created before the creator reached the age of forty. It happens fortunately for those who cling to this theory that many great poets have died and some have lost their reason before this crucial age, but the fact hardly warrants the conclusion that it would be better had such a fate overtaken them all. Let us hear upon this the opinion of one of our leading modern artists.[1] He is writing, it is true, of painting, but his words perhaps apply to every art:

But it must not be forgotten that good painters, like good wine, are apt to improve with age, and it is often the work of their later years which moves us most to admiration. Perhaps it is not till an artist is turned fifty that he can be unreservedly accepted. By that time, it is true, he will have shed the pleasant attributes of youth but will have preserved undimmed its inner vision and, with the experience of a lifetime, be on the way to grasp at last the long-sought magical formula by means of which he will be able to achieve that perfect fusion of his soul with external nature which is the touchstone of the greatest art. Doubtless he will have become in the process rather difficult to

[1] Augustus John, R.A., *The Unknown Artist* (in *Vogue*, March 7, 1928).

handle and maybe almost impossible to understand, for he will
necessarily have withdrawn himself somewhat apart from a
world

> *Where Charity is made a Trade that men grow rich by,*
> *And the Sandy Desert is given to the Strong.*

It is greatly to be desired that every one who approaches
Goethe—and more especially *Faust*—might be forced to
digest Mr. John's words before light-heartedly setting out to
pillory the weaknesses they so easily discern in the works of
the poet's old age. When they find him, as they so often do,
'rather difficult to handle' and, frequently, 'almost impossible
to understand' they may then—with Mr. John's assistance—
perhaps begin again the baffling process of the search for
'the touchstone' of the poet's art. Hitherto they have preferred, as a rule, to take a shorter way with Goethe. They
have contented themselves with, more or less inadequately,
appreciating his 'message' and, fairly definitely, refusing to
take seriously the question of his art.

Lest it be thought that I exaggerate, let me cite a characteristic specimen of English criticism of Goethe by an anonymous, but obviously thoughtful, critic.[1] The very title of the
essay seems in itself to announce the writer's feeling that
Goethe's art is not a matter of great moment, contrasted with
his culture and his religion. Having carefully stressed the
'strange and perverse mixture of the noble and the petty'
in the poet's character, the critic adds:

In his art, too, we find the same old contradiction. Few men
have ever more deeply felt the purity and nobility of Greek art
than Goethe, yet this did not prevent him from filling his longer
works, such as *Wilhelm Meister*, *Faust*, and *Die Wahlverwandt-
schaften*, with amorphous masses of matter which he was determined to unload somewhere, and by which the design was

---

[1] *The Gospel of Goethe.* Leading article in *The Times Literary Supplement* for
December 9, 1920 (No. 986). The article was occasioned by the appearance
of the late Professor Hume Brown's *Life of Goethe* in two volumes (London,
1920). I have revised the orthography and typographical peculiarities of the
original.

completely swamped. *Iphigenie* is, perhaps, the only important work of Goethe's in which the lessons of Greece are faithfully applied.

Such is the traditional uncritical-critical English method of dismissing Goethe's maturest works.[1] We need scarcely wonder that the Germans laugh at our cocksure *pronunciamentos* and uninterested conceptions of an art which we do not appear even to care to examine. Like Wagner, the pedant *famulus*, these English critics seem to have jumped to the conclusion that the master was 'declaiming a Greek tragedy', and they feel hurt, puzzled, and annoyed when they discover things far more strange and unfamiliar. Wagner has indeed had, to cite Croce, 'a long, varied, and honest progeny' of persons who will never recognize that the kind of 'perfection' they are seeking is, in general, 'a dead thing, an abstraction'. It is, after all, only a Wagnerian pedant—with little appreciation of either history or psychology—who can long to find in *Faust* 'the lessons of Greece faithfully applied'. For *Faust* is, among other things, the outstanding symbol of modern poetry precisely because it is written in many moods about one vast theme and ends in an upward-tending but somewhat indistinct gesture rather than in a dogmatic epilogue. Unending progress, not the certain reward of a golden throne among the gods of Greece, nor the tragedy of a noble but hopeless struggle with Ananke, is the fate of the symbolic hero. And the form of the work is *necessarily* no more 'Greek' than the content.

[1] F. W. H. in *The Manchester Guardian* for April 10, 1929, strikes a somewhat more cheerful note, but also insists upon the 'piecing together of the Second Part, which . . . is so very different from the fine rapture of the First Part, completed thirty years before.' (The exaggeration to *thirty* is again typical.)

II. *The Magical Formula*

> Und steh beschämt, wenn du bekennen musst:
> Ein guter Mensch in seinem dunklen Drange
> Ist sich des rechten Weges wohl bewusst.
> *(Faust, Prolog im Himmel, 327–9.)*

> Er überwächst uns schon
> An mächtigen Gliedern;
> Wird treuer Pflege Lohn
> Reichlich erwidern . . . *(Faust II, 12076–9.)*

One grows weary of the captious critics with their scalpels
and excisions. Let us grant them the truth—or platitude—
of their main contention. Goethe's *Faust* contains over 12,000
lines; like the city of Rome and the British Constitution it
was not made in a day, and from no point of view, even that
of Mr. Augustus John's touchstone of the 'fusion' of the poet's
soul 'with external nature', can it be considered perfect.
As Goethe himself remarked, 'Alles Menschenwerk ist Stück-
werk'. Anyone who cares to dig them out can find in Goethe's
own letters and conversations plenty of ammunition to hurl
at those who dare to claim artistic unity for this poem. But
the captious critics have grown so bold that they deny, of
course under Goethe's aegis, the philosophic value of the
work. One of them,[1] himself too careless to cite correctly
the two most familiar lines from *Faust*, solemnly informs us
that '*Faust* is poetry, not thought', and naïvely adds, 'and
Goethe was never weary of driving home that point'. Alas,
poor Goethe! And the great Croce himself can certainly
be invoked in support, for has he not committed, among
other indiscretions, that of pronouncing the Prologue in
Heaven to be 'the jest of a great artist, but not more than a
jest, quite out of harmony with the drama which follows and

[1] The writer of the leading article on Goethe in *The Times Literary Supplement*
for December 20, 1923, which is partly a review of Croce's very unequal little
volume on Goethe, to which allusion is made below. *The Times* expert's version of the famous lines is:
> *Wer stets bestrebend sich bemüht*
> *Den können wir erlösen.*
The broadest-backed printer can scarcely be blamed for this!

which was, in the first period, planned to be serious; a scene in Paradise with the angels, God, and the devil, where there is not even an archaic colouring, but a *dégagé* manner, slightly in the style of Voltaire'. Alas, poor Goethe-Yorick-Voltaire!

Reader, close your Croce, open your Goethe! Have these critics ever tried to realize the meaning of that great song of the archangels, with which the Prologue in Heaven opens, which strikes the key-note of the whole poem and contains—no matter how many immature students and over-ripe critics miss the patent fact—a whole theodicy in twenty-eight brief lines? If not a vindication, it is most assuredly a magnificent asseveration of Divine Providence in view of the existence of evil. Most readers of *Faust* hurry through it as though it *were* a mere deliberate piece of decorative archaism. They would find it instructive to ponder every line of these magnificent chants, to read them aloud and translate them carefully, preferably for someone who knows no German. Few will find it a very easy task. Almost no one, having performed it, will ever again pass over these lines as 'mere poetry', great poetry as they are. At the risk of seeming pedantic I reprint them here:

### PROLOG IM HIMMEL

Der Herr, die himmlischen Heerscharen, *nachher* Mephistopheles.[1] Die drei Erzengel treten vor.

#### RAPHAEL

Die Sonne tönt nach alter Weise
In Brudersphären Wettgesang,
Und ihre vorgeschriebene Reise
Vollendet sie mit Donnergang.

---

[1] How many English readers ever notice this *nachher*, by which the 'Prolog im Himmel' is clearly divided into two (strictly three) scenes? It has for some time been my custom to get my pupils to translate these twenty-eight lines and then treat them as the French have their classics treated by the method of *lecture expliquée*. The results are often most enlightening to both pupil and teacher.

Ihr Anblick gibt den Engeln Stärke,
Wenn keiner sie ergründen mag:
Die unbegreiflich hohen Werke
Sind herrlich wie am ersten Tag.

GABRIEL

Und schnell und unbegreiflich schnelle
Dreht sich umher der Erde Pracht:
Es wechselt Paradieses-Helle
Mit tiefer, schauervoller Nacht:
Es schäumt das Meer in breiten Flüssen
Am tiefen Grund der Felsen auf,
Und Fels und Meer wird fortgerissen
In ewig schnellem Sphärenlauf.

MICHAEL

Und Stürme brausen um die Wette,
Vom Meer aufs Land, vom Land aufs Meer,
Und bilden wütend eine Kette
Der tiefsten Wirkung rings umher.
Da flammt ein blitzendes Verheeren
Dem Pfade vor des Donnerschlags—
Doch deine Boten, Herr, verehren
Das sanfte Wandeln deines Tags.

ZU DREI

Der Anblick gibt den Engeln Stärke,
Da keiner dich ergründen mag,
Und alle deine hohen Werke
Sind herrlich wie am ersten Tag.

The second portion of the Prologue, which Signor Croce
finds Voltairean (for even he could hardly write thus of the
lines just quoted), is of course based upon the famous scene
in the Book of Job. That, however, is so familiar a fact that
to dwell upon it would only retard us unnecessarily. There
is more excuse for insisting upon the meaning and importance of the archangels' song. It is surely intended to assert,
and does so assert in splendid poetry, instinct with thought,
that the Universe not only was created, but is sustained by

one living, all-powerful Creator, whose will and purpose may be discerned in the 'high works' of his hand, in the dark and terrific, as in the light and paradisiac—*discerned, not plumbed to the depths.* These works are too high for the minds of the created to grasp in their fullness and depth, even their movements are too swift for the created mind to seize and follow; their alternations of violence and gentleness, of murk and brilliance, startling to the minds even of the angels, are part of their Creator's will and purpose, of the integrated unity of creation.

> The very storms do race and roar
> From sea to land and land to sea,
> And raging form an endless chain
> Of deep causation round the earth.

We have been lightly assured that *Faust* is 'poetry, not thought'. The facile, specious distinction breaks down almost at the first lines of the great poem. No intelligent reader would expect to find in *Faust* a treatise on philosophy even faintly resembling the *Kritik der reinen Vernunft*, but why this futile attempt to dissever poetry, especially this poem, from thought? On the contrary, *Faust* is just as much rooted in thought as in feeling, though the one may predominate in this section of the poem and the other in that. And, to do them justice, even the disintegrators generally admit the existence of an *idée maîtresse*, a *Leitgedanke*, though some of them, like Croce, will have it that the hero of the Second Part is a different being from him of the First. As a matter of fact, established by research, the *Leitgedanke* or guiding conception of *Faust* may be directly traced—it has been recently traced by Konrad Burdach, the most learned Germanist alive—to no less philosophic a writer than Leibniz.[1]

---

[1] The remarkable similarity of the *Weltanschauungen* of Goethe and Leibniz seems to have long escaped notice, owing perhaps principally to Goethe's own expressed interest in Spinoza. The similarity is brought out clearly in Dietrich Mahnke's study *Leibniz und Goethe, Die Harmonie ihrer Weltansichten* (*Weisheit und Tat*, herausgegeben von Arthur Hoffmann, Heft 4: Erfurt, 1924). Mahnke

The passage in which Burdach[1] finds, and seems justified in finding, the 'Grundgedanke' of Goethe's *Faust* occurs in Leibniz' *Vernünftige Grundsätze von der Natur und der Gnade* (at page 781 of the edition of 1744). It is so striking and so clearly echoed in *Faust* that no argument seems necessary to prove that it was indeed the chief rock upon which the philosophy, or rather the theology, of *Faust* came to be grounded. As it may not be readily obtained by all my readers I repeat it here, as cited by Burdach:

> Es ist wahr, die höchste Glückseligkeit, sie sey gleich mit irgend einem *seligmachenden Anschauen*, oder einer Erkenntnis Gottes verbunden, wie sie wolle, kann niemals vollkommen seyn: indem Gott, da er unendlich ist, nicht gänzlich erkannt werden kann. Also wird und muss auch unsere Glückseligkeit *niemals in einem völligen Genusse* bestehen, *dabey weiter nichts zu wünschen übrig bliebe*, und wo unser Geist stumpf werden könnte: sondern in einem *beständigen Fortgange*, von Ergetzungen und *neuen Vollkommenheiten*.

Burdach points out that this confession of faith is also 'that truth, which allows the Lord God to win his wager with Mephistopheles, the secret cause of the perpetual state of dissatisfaction, of ever renewed desire and ceaselessly striving toil, that masters Faust up to his last moment on earth and prepares for him the way for his future climb upwards to God'.

It might content us to leave the matter here, asserting with Burdach that Leibniz supplies Goethe with the theo-

at p. 13 calls attention to the fact that Gottsched's German edition of Leibniz' *Théodicée* (and other works) was to be found in the library of Goethe's father in Frankfurt-am-Main. He quotes part of the same passage as is cited by Burdach and compares Faust's words 'kannst du mich mit Genuss betrügen', &c. Mahnke and Burdach appear to have arrived independently at the same conclusion, but Burdach in his *Faust und Moses* (1912) took this line earlier.

[1] *Die Disputationsszene und die Grundidee in Goethes Faust.* Von Konrad Burdach. In the periodical *Euphorion*, 27 Band, Erstes Heft (Stuttgart, 1926), pp. 1–69. The passage in question is cited at page 59. Burdach's earlier extremely important essay on *Faust und Moses* appeared in the 'Sitzungsberichte der kgl. Preussischen Akademie der Wissenschaften' in 1912 (Nos. xxiii, xxxv, and xxxviii). The *Euphorion* essay is an expansion of earlier work dating from 1916.

logical formula for *Faust*, the poet's part being to supply the magic which turns dogma into art, but the perennial interest of the work invites us to further analysis. We have seen that that formula of the 'Gehalt' of *Faust* is theological, but, deriving immediately from Leibniz, it might be considered 'modern'. Before we go on to the 'Gestalt' let us, however, note as clearly as may be that, despite its Storm-and-Stress remnants, its classical elements, and its neo-platonic affinities, *Faust*, for all its seeming modernity and its Leibnizian formula, is the last great poetic version of the scholastic *Weltanschauung*. It turns essentially upon the most burning question of medieval philosophic theology, the question of man's imperfection and man's perfectibility. This is a question which would seem to have exercised the mind of Goethe from an early age up to the very end of his life. It does not seem to be sufficiently remarked how close Goethe appears to come in *Faust*—especially in the scenes following Faust's death—to the theology of the *Doctor angelicus*, Thomas Aquinas.[1]

We know from Eckermann[2] which verses Goethe regarded as containing the 'Schlüssel zu Fausts Rettung'. We are perhaps nowadays a little too ready to stress Faust's 'immer höhere und reinere Tätigkeit bis ans Ende', and forget that Goethe added the words 'und von oben die ihm zu Hilfe kommende ewige Liebe'. The sentence which follows ends with a phrase that points back perhaps not only to the New Testament, especially to the Revelation of St. John the Divine,[3] but also to Thomas Aquinas' doctrine of the 'king-

---

[1] R. Petsch refers only to Franz von Assisi in connexion with the *Pater seraphicus*, but this title belongs also to Bonaventura, to whom Goethe may also be indebted. In Goethe, as in Leibniz, we have the same combination as in Nicolas of Cusa, *coincidentia oppositorum*, 'Mystik und Aufklärung zugleich', as E. Bergmann says of Nicolas (*Gesch. d. deutschen Philos.*, I. Bd.: *Die deutsche Mystik*, Breslau, 1926, p. 62). [2] *Gespräche mit Goethe*, June 6, 1831. [3] Cf. in Luther's version *Rev.* i. 4: Gnade sey mit euch, und friede vom dem, der da ist, und der da war, und der da kömmt, und von den sieben geistern, die da sind vor seinem stuhl; and *Rev.* ii. 7 f. : Wer überwindet, dem will ich

dom of grace' which perfects the 'kingdom of things'. Goethe says:

> Es steht dieses mit unserer religiösen Vorstellung durchaus in Harmonie, nach welcher wir nicht bloss durch eigene Kraft selig werden, sondern durch die hinzukommende göttliche Gnade.

In the *Prolog im Himmel* Goethe had long since confronted his readers with a hierarchy of spirits of different degrees of perfection and imperfection, God, the archangels and angels, *the* or *a* devil Mephistopheles, and the man Faust, the destined object of the proposed contest. 'Inter theologicos libros *Summa theologiae* eminet, summis laudibus celebrata.' Goethe, who claims to have read Brucker's History of Philosophy[1] diligently in his youth, can scarcely have overlooked the greatest of the Schoolmen, though he may be indebted more directly to Leibniz, Campanella, and other intermediaries. It is in the seventy-seventh question of the first part of the *Summa theologica* that Thomas poses the inquiry *Utrum sint plures potentiae animae* and answers thus:

> Respondeo dicendum quod necesse est ponere plures animae potentias.
>
> . . . Dicendum est ergo, quod res, quae sunt infra hominem, quaedam particularia bona consequuntur: et ideo quasdam paucas et determinatas operationes habent et virtutes. Homo autem potest consequi universalem et perfectam bonitatem, quia

zu essen geben von dem holtz des lebens, das im paradiess Gottes ist . . . Sey getreu bis an den tod, so will ich dir die krone des lebens geben . . . Wer überwindet, dem soll kein leid geschehen von dem andern tode.—Goethe himself takes credit for having given his 'poetischen Intentionen' both 'Form und Festigkeit' by introducing these 'scharf umrissenen christlich-kirchlichen Figuren und Vorstellungen' (Eckermann, *ibid.*). Petsch remarks, 'Von einem innerlich "katholisierenden" Schluss kann keine Rede sein'; but the influence of Christian mysticism on the whole poem and notably on the 'Schluss' seems undeniable. Goethe perhaps owed more to Herder than is commonly supposed.
[1] See Jac. Bruckeri *Hist. Crit. Philos.*, tom. iii (1743), p. 807, and Goethe's *Einwirkung der neueren Philosophie* (1820), Jubiläums-Ausg., Bd. 39, p. 29, and *ibid.*, p. 354 for Goethe's quotation from Thomas Campanella. The articles on Campanella in Brucker's work show him to have been in fairly close agreement with Aquinas on the most essential points. (See vol. v, pp. 142–4, and especially vol. vi (1767), pp. 827–30 with the final vindication: 'atheismi turpitudine cumulandus haud est'.)

potest adipisci beatitudinem. Est tamen in ultimo gradu secundum naturam eorum quibus competit beatitudo: et ideo multis et diversis operationibus et virtutibus indiget anima humana. Angelis vero minor diversitas potentiarum competit. In Deo vero non est aliqua potentia, vel actio praeter ejus essentiam.

Est et alia ratio quare anima humana abundat diversitate potentiarum, videlicet quia est in confinio spiritualium et corporalium creaturarum; et ideo concurrunt in ipsa virtutes utrarumque creaturarum.

Ad primum ergo dicendum quod in hoc ipso magis ad similitudinem Dei accedit anima intellectiva quam creaturae inferiores, quod perfectam bonitatem consequi potest, licet per multa et diversa: in quo deficit a superioribus.[1]

Morhof, in his *Polyhistor* (ii. 85), writes of Thomas Aquinas as 'Alpha Scholasticorum . . . Vocatur *plus, quam Salomon, Interpres divinae voluntatis, matutinus Lucifer, quasi Luna sapientia & moribus, & veluti Sol oriens mundo.*' It would be strange if Goethe had never been moved to gain a first-hand acquaintance with the *Doctor Angelicus*, but it would still not greatly matter; the exact degree of his dependence upon Aquinas or any intermediary is, for us, secondary. Goethe claimed to be, after all, chiefly an artist ('Künstler'), and what matters for us is to realize the difference that this philosophy of God, man, angels, and devils made to his art in *Faust*. His method

---

[1] *S. Theol.* Pars Prima, Quaestio LXXVII, art. ii (vol. i, col. 1088 of the ed. published by J.-P. Migne, Paris, 1841, along with P. Lombardi *Sententiae*). In Quaestio CXII (*ibid.* i, 1363) Aquinas discusses the appearance of Satan before God, as related in *Job* i. 6, under the heading (art. iii) *Utrum omnes Angeli qui mittuntur, assistant*. His conclusion is 'quod Satan non dicitur adstitisse [coram Deo], sed inter assistentes adfuisse describitur; quia, ut Gregorius dicit 2 Moral., cap. 2., circ. fin., *etsi beatitudinem perdidit, naturam tamen Angelis similem non amisit*'. This is a hint which a modern producer of *Faust* on the stage might do well to bear in mind. Why not present Mephistopheles as a 'feiner junger Geselle' (to use Luther's phrase) similar to Raphael in the book of Tobit? In Quaestio CXIV, *De daemonum impugnatione* (art. ii, *ibid.* 1377), Aquinas throws some light on the 'wager' between God and Mephistopheles: 'daemones sciunt ea quae exterius aguntur circa homines; sed interiorem hominis conditionem solus Deus novit, qui est spirituum ponderator; ex qua aliqui sunt magis proni ad unum vitium quam ad aliud. Et ideo diabolus tentat explorando interiorem conditionem hominis, ut de illo vitio tentet ad quod homo magis pronus est.'

of producing his commentary on life is that of employing *phantasmata*; he is the nearest German successor to Dürer, despite the gap in time between them. And in *Faust*, at least, his artistic 'Einstellung' is far more Gothic than Greek. In a true sense Goethe was 'the heir of all the ages', but in *Faust* his 'tiefreligiöse Natur', as Jakob Minor called it,[1] anti-dogmatic though it clearly is, rests after all upon the conception of 'Hinaufstreben in den Himmel Gottes' in the midst of this confusing earthly world, which he makes Christ address with the words

> O Welt voll wunderbaarer Wirrung,
> Voll Geist der Ordnung, träger Irrung,
> Du Kettenring von Wonn und Wehe,
> Du Mutter, die mich selbst zum Grab gebahr!
> Die ich, obgleich ich bey der Schöpfung war,
> Im ganzen doch nicht sonderlich verstehe.
> Die Dumpfheit deines Sinns, in der du schwebtest,
> Daraus du dich nach meinem Tage drangst,
> Die Schlangenknotige Begier, in der du bebtest,
> Von ihr dich zu befreyen strebtest,
> Und dann befreyt dich wieder neu umschlangst,
> Das rief mich her aus meinem Sternen Saale
> Das lässt mich nicht an Gottes Busen ruhn.
> Ich komme nun zu dir zum zweiten male,
> Ich säete dann und erndten will ich nun.[2]

This conception is biblical and—let us pronounce the word boldly—'Gothic' rather than classical. But this word Gothic

---

[1] *Goethes Fragmente vom ewigen Juden, &c.* (Stuttgart and Berlin, 1904), p. 211. Cf. *ibid.*, pp. 42 f., 58, 93 f.

[2] Goethe's fragment *Der wiederkehrende Heiland* (Jacob Minor, *op. cit.*, pp. 95–6). As Minor takes pains to point out, Goethe has just described the Devil as 'Freund Satanas' in the same humorous tone in which he makes God and Mephistopheles converse in the *Faust* Prologue. Cf. *ibid.*, p. 99, ' "Freud' muss Leid, Leid muss Freude haben", wie es im Faust heisst.' It may be true, as Minor adds (*ibid.*, p. 100), that even the Second Part of *Faust* has no passage 'von gleich religiöser Gewalt' to set beside this early fragment, but my point is that the underlying conception is still the same. The lines 'Du Kettenring von Wonn und Wehe' and 'Die ich . . . doch nicht sonderlich verstehe' seem to be clearly echoed by the archangels in the *Prolog im Himmel*.

brings us at last to the question of form. What we have still to say of the 'Gehalt' may be dealt with while we say what needs to be said of the 'Gestalt' of Goethe's masterpiece.

We have seen that the thought-formula is religious, even theological. It derives from the Old Testament, the New Testament, the Greek Pantheon, Plato, Aristotle, Plotinus, the Moses legend (Gregory of Nyssa), the Koran, Gottfried Arnold, the Pietists, Leibniz, no less than from the traditional accounts of Faust, Paracelsus, and other magicians. If we have ventured to lay special stress upon St. Thomas Aquinas as the forerunner of Leibniz and Goethe, it is because in him we find the clearest formulation of the theological and ethical conceptions underlying both Goethe's *Faust* and the Gothic spirit in art, of which it was (in 1833) the last and greatest product. 'Die künstlerische Formung und Beseelung der deutschen Poesie und ihrer Sprache, die das 18. Jahrhundert gebracht hat', says Burdach,[1] 'wurzelt *in religiöser Erregung des Gefühls und der Phantasie*, mit der eng verwachsen ist der Drang nach Annäherung an *die Musik*', to which he adds the highly significant footnote, 'Ebenso wie die Renaissance des 13. und 14. Jahrhunderts.'

It is a good while now since Erich Schmidt in his introduc-

[1] *Faust und Moses*, 3. Teil (*loc. cit.*, p. 741). In *Faust*, as in the nearest and grandest late medieval parallel, Johannes von Saaz's prose-dialogue *Der Ackermann aus Böhmen*, we have a meeting-place of medieval theology and modern humanism. Of *Der Ackermann* Burdach (*Vorspiel*, i. Bd., 2. Teil, p. 220) remarks: 'Durch das Ganze geht ein unkirchlicher, aber nicht kirchenfeindlicher Zug, und absichtsvoll enthält sich die Schlusslitanei des Witwers für das Seelenheil der Frau jeder Anrufung der Heiligen und der Jungfrau Maria.' Goethe, on the other hand, makes free artistic use of the Madonna concept (*Mater gloriosa, Doctor Marianus, Chorus mysticus*). Theodor Däubler in his brilliant but cryptic discussion of *Faust* (*Sparta, ein Versuch*, Leipzig, 1923, p. 31) surely is misled in suggesting that Proteus' lines to Homunculus (*Du bist ein wahrer Jungfernsohn, Eh du sein solltest, bist du schon!* [Teil II, 8253–4]) prove 'Dass die Walpurgisnacht ein Hohn auf den Himmel, eine Art Satansmesse (ist)'. Even if they refer to the Madonna they do not express the poet's own outlook and, at most, are a jest in doubtful taste. On the other hand, that Goethe even here should introduce the Madonna-concept would go to show his preoccupation with this figure.

tion to the Jubiläums-Ausgabe of *Faust* described this Faust
as 'diese symbolischeste Gestalt der ganzen germanischen
Poesie', but hardly yet is it readily admitted that Faust is
throughout the same Faust, and is throughout symbolic.
Goethe himself is partly responsible. In the First Part he
made great, indeed excessive, concessions to Naturalism, one
result being that, as in *Götz* the role of Adelheid, so here the
role of Gretchen tends to be over-stressed—of course to the
joy of the romantic-realistic school of critics. In the Second
Part he did not hesitate, in a neo-baroque manner, to indulge
in all sorts of 'classical' excursions which, at times, weary or
mystify even patient readers and, worse still, strike them as
spoiling what might have been a creditable counterpart to
the truly classical dramas of Ancient Greece. The reader
does not easily realize that what he has before him is a Gothic
edifice, because his mind keeps wandering to the baroque
additions, or even prefers to rest on the 'romantic' and
'human' story of Faust and Gretchen.

It is easy to call *Faust* Gothic, less easy to offer some
reasoned argument for so calling it. The mere fact that this
work is at once intensely religious and supremely human does
not help us far, for the same may be said of the highest types
of Greek art or literature. The key to the problem lies rather
in the formal aspect of the work, since the form is the
expression of the spirit, the spirit made manifest to the senses.
For man, at least, nothing exists without form, however
simplified: form, we say, is characteristic. (We say the same
thing of the thought, but the thought cannot be expressed
without taking shape, if only in a gesture. 'So-and-so', we say,
'said nothing, but made a characteristic gesture.')

What then is characteristic at once of *Faust* and of Gothic
art? I can but briefly suggest the answer. The least misleading expression of their similarity might appear to some
to be ultra-dogmatic. The formula would be to the effect
that as artistic products of the human spirit they both appear

less anthropocentric and more 'theovert', if one may coin the term, than do the classics. The Greeks and Romans, on the whole, tended to make their gods in the image of themselves, only grander and more powerful. The medieval Christians, reversing the process, regarded God as the One from whom emanated and to whom aspired the men and women created by him as 'Ebenbilder' of Himself. The leading concepts of their religions inevitably reacted upon the artists of the two periods. Their 'values' in art tended to take their distinctive tones from their religious 'orientation'. Form and substance of the true work of art emanate alike from the creative spirit of the artist, to which the substance is subdued and by which it is endued with form. *Faust* bears the stamp of one creator, whose orientation, in the last resort, is more akin to that of St. Thomas Aquinas and therefore to the Gothic than to the more anthropocentric Greek minds, despite many apparently contradictory signs. The Stoics and the neo-Platonists, to both of whom Goethe is indebted, may be reckoned as intermediate types. Our endeavour is by no means to set up a rigid dichotomy.

The difference may be seen most clearly in the attitudes of these artists towards idealism on the one hand and naturalism on the other. In neither period is there any question of an absolute rule holding good throughout, but comparing the ancient with the medieval, and much of the modern, art we seem to recognize in the latter, upon the whole, a change in the point of view, which could not have occurred but for 'die Werke der grossen mittelalterlichen Denker, für die das Problem der Stellung der Menschen zu gewaltigen geistigen Abstraktionen und die durch sie bedingte Auffassung der Welt der Sinne durch Jahrhunderte der Mittelpunkt der geistigen Interessen gewesen ist'.[1] We

[1] Max Dvořák, 'Idealismus und Naturalismus in der gotischen Skulptur und Malerei', *Historische Zeitschrift*, Bd. 119 (München und Berlin, 1919), pp. 9–10. This long and profound essay (*ibid.*, pp. 1–62 and 185–246), since reissued in book form, is perhaps the most important study of the principles and

observe, first and foremost, in the early middle ages a 'concentration of the interests upon supernatural truths',[1] which tends, upon the whole, to lead in art to the victory of idealism over naturalism.

But in all periods development is the law of life. Naturalism, banned almost wholly from the earliest medieval art, could not be banished completely from the philosophical analysis of a world of sensible forms and objects. 'Das Leben erhielt', in the course of time and thought, 'einen neuen Eigenwert als Schauplatz verdienstvoller Werke, die Natur eine neue Bedeutung als das Zeugnis der Allmacht und Weisheit Gottes'.[2] And once more art reflected the new *Weltanschauung*, in which the visible, sensible, intelligible world about man was looked upon as the 'Spiegel des Absoluten, Ewigen, Unendlichen' and as simply the 'Manifestation des sensuell und rationell unfassbaren göttlichen Gedankens'.[3]

It is impossible to follow here the development of this *Weltanschauung* in Gothic art; the reader who desires to do so may be recommended to study the process in Dvořák's illuminating pages. The most essential fact is that, while naturalism is no longer excluded from the artist's mind, that mind consciously substitutes for 'truth to nature' and 'imitation of nature' a higher and more spiritual conception of the artist's task and mission. For him nature is the garment of God, the world is divinely ordered, but to the artist is given the higher insight into the mind of the Creator and the privilege of mirroring this mind more closely than does the reflection of it obtained through the 'dark glass' of his senses by the ordinary man. Accordingly, in both form and content, subjectivity and spirituality asserted their right to dominate over the mere desire to do justice to the outward appearances

---

development of Gothic sculpture and painting hitherto made public. For myself I owe to it any understanding I may have of this—to my mind the least easily intelligible—period of European art. My remarks on the Gothic are based upon this essay of Dvořák's.

[1] *Ibid.*, p. 186.          [2] *Ibid.*, p. 15.          [3] *Ibid.*, p. 20.

of the visible and tangible objects presented by nature to the senses. Art became more abstract and the attitude of the artist to his product became more sovereign, as he became more and more conscious of his insight into the mind of the Creator. Selection of that which is vitally important, from this spiritual point of view, became the artist's guiding rule. He did not set out to produce an *imago* of nature, but rather a more perfect specimen of the underlying spiritual concept, he was guided by one of St. Thomas Aquinas's leading doctrines, *Pulchritudo habet claritatem*,[1] which means, in part at least, that the unimportant must be sacrificed. On the other hand, since *integritas*, or completeness, was also demanded, a certain degree of naturalism was not shut out, but actually and explicitly required. The necessity of holding that balance between the two demands resulted in the third demand, that for *consonantia*, becoming all-important. The best medieval artists aimed at and frequently achieved an ideal harmony between their spiritual concepts and the material objects they presented.

It may, of course, be urged that a somewhat similar harmony is to be found in the Greek art of the fifth century B.C. But there the emphasis is different, because the underlying temper and *Weltanschauung* are less spiritual and less monotheistic. The very struggle of the Gothic to admit a certain degree of naturalism is self-conscious, and the stress laid upon the necessity for it proves, as Dvořák says,[2] 'wie weit man grundsätzlich von der Antike entfernt war und wie sehr das Verhältnis der Kunst zur Natur und zum Leben ein anderes geworden ist'. It was not now a simple struggle between idealism and naturalism, but an effort to deal justly with the claims of both under the 'Primat einer spirituell idealistischen Weltkonstruktion', which rendered such a synthesis not merely desirable but inevitable. But whereas in classical art the

[1] For this and other relevant passages from St. Thomas cf. Dvořák, *loc. cit.*, pp. 37 f. The idea of *consonantia*, as suggested by St. Thomas, is analysed and elaborated at pp. 39 ff.          [2] *Ibid.*, pp. 38 f.

norm had been established *from without*, it was now re-established *from within*. 'Der Unterschied bestand vor allem darin, dass sich *die Objektivität vom Objekt in das Subjekt verschoben hat.*'[1] But this did not imply the reign of individualism, because of the prevailing doctrine of 'general spiritual truths' revealed in special measure to the artists and propounded in the works of art.

To follow out in detail the effects of this spiritual 'Einstellung' would carry us too far, though it might throw further light on our subject. It is necessary, however, to record the admission that the principle of naturalism once having regained recognition was difficult to control. The contradiction between naturalism and idealism tended to become more and more marked, as the generations of Gothic artists succeeded one another, so that we even remark at last 'das Streben nach Überwindung jeder Norm' establishing itself as characteristic of the Gothic naturalism.[2]

The very phrase reminds us of the Goethe of the *Shakespearrede*, the essay *Von deutscher Baukunst*, and the *Urfaust*, as they appear in the common tradition of literary histories. 'Schädlicher als Beyspiele sind dem Genius Principien.' Undeniably Goethe himself says it.[3] 'Schule und Prinzipium fesselt—' But what? 'Schule und Principium fesselt *alle Kraft der Erkenntnis und Tätigkeit*'. . . . 'So vermag keiner deiner Schlüsse *sich zur Region der Wahrheit zu erheben*. . .'—'Da offenbarte sich mir, in leisen Ahndungen, der Genius des grossen Werkmeisters. Was staunst du? lispelt' er mir entgegen. Alle diese Massen waren *notwendig*, und siehst du sie nicht an allen älteren Kirchen meiner Stadt? Nur ihre *willkürliche* Grössen hab ich *zum stimmenden Verhältnis erhoben* . . .'

---

[1] *Ibid.*, pp. 40–1, where stress is also laid upon that other side of the Gothic art which arises in the 'Bestreben durch bildliche Erfindungen Gefühle und Vorstellungen einer vollständigen Loslösung vom realen Sein zugunsten eines übermateriellen geistigen Geschehens zu erwecken.' (Cf. Goethe's 'Gefühl ist alles', &c., *Faust* I, 3456.)    [2] Dvořák, *ibid.*, p. 208.
[3] Cf. Goethe, *Von deutscher Baukunst* (D. M. Ervini a Steinbach), 1772 (Jub. Ausg. Bd. 33, pp. 5–9).

He delights to 'schauen die grossen *harmonischen Massen*, zu unzählig kleinen Teilen belebt; wie in Werken der ewigen Natur, bis aufs geringste Zäserchen, *alles Gestalt, und alles zweckend zum Ganzen . . .*'

The essay *Von deutscher Baukunst* is rather dithyrambic and it is not thought out to the end. The way is left open even for 'Bildnerei aus den willkürlichsten Formen', 'sie wird ohne Gestaltsverhältnis zusammenstimmen', we are told: 'denn *eine* Empfindung schuf sie zum charakteristischen Ganzen'. But again we are assured there are degrees of virtue in art, as produced by different peoples and individuals, in fact 'unzählige Grade'. There are 'Verhältnisse, die allein schön und von Ewigkeit sind', which the soul must raise itself up to feel; the secrets of these relationships can only be felt, but their 'Hauptakkorde' can be proved. The life of the 'Genius' is a dance performed to the blessed melodies of these relationships, but he has a definite, in fact the highest possible, character, he is 'gottgleich'; and

'je mehr diese Schönheit in das Wesen eines Geistes eindringt, dass sie mit ihm entstanden zu sein scheint, dass ihm nichts genugtut als sie, dass er nichts aus sich wirkt als sie; desto glücklicher ist der Künstler, desto herrlicher ist er, desto tiefgebeugter stehen wir da und beten an *den Gesalbten Gottes.*'[1]

We need not insist that Goethe here lays down in the clearest language the divine origin of the true artist's inspiration. What though he work 'aus starker, rauher, deutscher Seele, auf dem eingeschränkten düstern Pfaffenschauplatz des medii aevi', Erwin has climbed to a height from which none can throw him down. 'Hier steht sein Werk, tretet hin und erkennt das tiefste Gefühl von Wahrheit und Schönheit der Verhältnisse. . . .' It is necessary to insist that even now

[1] Goethe, *op. cit.*, *ibid.*, p. 11. This idea is, of course, by no means original. Goethe may be echoing Shaftesbury or some earlier critic. Cf. the views of Caspar Barth on Homer, cited at pp. 110–11 of my *Hölderlin and the German Neo-Hellenic Movement*, Part I, with those of Shaftesbury in his *Soliloquy* (1710) (*ibid.*, p. 121, footnote 2). E. Maass, *Goethe und die Antike*, p. 82, stresses the classical origin of Goethe's view.

in 1772, and under the strong influence of Herder, Goethe does not refuse 'to know', though he puts 'to feel' first. My power, he says, unfolded itself full of delight 'zugleich zu geniessen und zu erkennen!'[1] He emphasizes and praises the 'Notwendigkeit, stimmendes Verhältnis, Schönheit, kühne schlanke Gestalt' of the work and the 'Wonneruh des Geistes, der auf solch eine Schöpfung herabschauen und gottgleich sprechen kann: Es ist gut!'[2] It would seem that, after all, supra-rationalism would be a better name than irrationalism for Goethe's state of mind at this time, for the God whom the artist resembles, and of whom man himself is called an 'Ebenbild', cannot well be thought of as an 'irrational' spirit, though his Being transcends, and sometimes makes foolishness of, the reasoning of man. Even Konrad Burdach went perhaps a little too far when he spoke of the 'trunkenen Enkomien' of the young Goethe 'auf den Erbauer des Strassburger Münsters'.[3] If Goethe's words are 'trunken', they are after all the words of a 'Gottbetrunkener', who has but newly realized to the full the affinity of man, and more especially of the great medieval German artist, with the Creator of the Universe. It is an inspiration apt to make any man of feeling, more still, a young, warm-hearted German poet of undoubted genius, talk in less sober tones than befit grave and learned men. Nor need we wonder when we hear Goethe echoing these tones 'auf jener menschlichen und künstlerischen Entwicklungsstufe, da er den Magier Faust den Erdgeist beschwören liess'.

We are not concerned here to support Burdach's thesis that the traditional (extra-biblical) legend concerning Moses was utilized by Goethe in his *Faust*. But one of his later statements[4] bears closely upon our main point.

'Die Moses-Sage', he assures us, 'hat mitnichten bloss den Abschluss der Fausttragödie beeinflusst. . . Auch der Faust, den die

---

[1] *Op. cit.*, p. 8.  [2] *Ibid.*, p. 9.
[3] Burdach, *Faust und Moses*, i. Teil, Sitzungsberichte der kgl. preuss. Akad. d. Wiss. (1912), xxii, p. 378.  [4] *Ibid.*, pp. 396–7.

Magie umstrickt, . . . auch er hat Elemente des Mosestypus. Und ebenso auch der Faust der früheren Entwicklungsstufe, der den Erdgeist beschwor, der auf den Brocken hinaufstürmte, der im Alpengebirge vor Sonnenaufgang die Einsicht gewann, die der entscheidende Schritt zur inneren Überwindung der Magie ist, die Einsicht, dass der Mensch das Sonnenlicht nicht unmittelbar, dass er es nur im farbigen Abglanz sehen und nur in diesem *das Leben* finden kann, die Einsicht, die der Sterbende wiederholt (v. 11,442 f.):

> Nach drüben ist die Aussicht uns verrannt:
> Tor, wer dorthin die Augen blinzelnd richtet.

Auch dieser Faust, der scheinbar vom Göttlichen sich abwendet, der es nur sucht in irdischer Tüchtigkeit und Tätigkeit, der es im Werden des Geschaffenen gewahrt, an dem seine Persönlichkeit eingreifend teilnimmt, auch er ist ein Abbild und allerdings auch ein Gegenbild jenes Moses, der im Laufe alter Traditionen der theosophischen Mystik, der magisch-pantheistischen christlichen und jüdischen Naturphilosophie aufgegangen war.'

The very heterogeneous character of this tradition need not detain us here, nor the importance of the Christian-neoplatonic transmission through Gregory of Nyssa. The essential point is that 'Der Berg des Moses' is 'das Wissen von Gott', yet on the topmost height of the holy place 'umfängt ihn von allen Seiten undurchsichtige und unbegreifliche Dunkelheit', even as he comes face to face with God.[1]

It would be idle to pretend that, at this period, Goethe's theology goes much beyond this vague Pantheism, or Panentheism. Yet even here he is so little 'kirchenfeindlich' as to make Gretchen answer

> Das ist alles recht schön und gut.
> Ohngefähr sagt das der Catechismus auch,
> Nur mit ein bisgen andern Worten.

But we are not now to examine the *Urfaust*, nor the later

---

[1] *Ibid.*, p. 398. Cf. p. 399, and *Urfaust*, 1123 ff., especially 1139–50, and Gretchen's reply. Behind the veil of sense, yet to be felt, the Almighty lives and moves, 'Unsichtbar-Sichtbar', 'und webt in ewigem Geheimnis'. 'Gefühl ist alles, Name Schall und Rauch, Umnebelnd Himmels Glut.'

*Fragment.* They are but stages, however important, in the growth of the finished work of art. Let us turn to this again and seek briefly to see it complete from the standpoint to which we have been led.

III. *The Completed Faust.*

We need not be pioneers, except perhaps to some extent in trying to win wider acceptance in England for a conception of *Faust* that of late years has made marked progress in Germany. This conception has been stated by Herr Heinrich Gerland [1] in uncompromising terms: '*So wie die Tragödie jetzt vorliegt, so hat sie Goethe als einheitliches Ganzes abgeschlossen und der Menschheit hinterlassen.*' Further, the 'Grundgedanke' is, in essentials, the same as in the beginning, however much the 'Ausführung' has been subject to change. The changes in the execution were many and remarkable. If we desire to see *Faust as a whole* we do best to disregard them for the time being. We have to learn to distinguish the historical from the descriptive method of analysis.

The idea of *Faust* is not simple, but complex. Every attempt to confine it within a single phrase or sentence is bound to break down. This is the meaning of Goethe's refusal, recorded by Eckermann,[2] to offer any brief reply to German inquirers who asked 'welche Idee ich in meinem *Faust* zu verkörpern gesucht'. His formulation of the 'Gang der Handlung' is brief indeed : '*Vom Himmel durch die Welt zur Hölle*' is, as he indicates, only 'zur Not etwas'. He, in fact, denies having consciously sought to incorporate any definite abstract concept in *Faust*, such as he has put in *Die Wahlver-*

---

[1] In *Logos*, Bd. XVI (1927), Heft 3, p. 260, in his essay entitled *Faust. Idee und Plan der Tragödie (ibid.*, pp. 259–86). In essentials the view is supported by Professor Heinrich Rickert. See especially his essay on *Die Einheit des Faustischen Charakters* in *Logos*, Bd. XIV, Heft 1 (1925), pp. 1–63. It is significant that Gerland's essay was written in 1895–6, but rejected by the editor of the *Goethe Jahrbücher* of that period.

[2] *Gespräche mit Goethe* (Sonntag den 6. Mai 1827).

*wandschaften*, and finally, in a phrase much easier to quote than to evaluate, expresses his opinion that 'je inkommensurabler und für den Verstand unfasslicher eine poetische Produktion, desto besser'. The faithful Eckermann naturally found no reply, and many another Goethe-*famulus* has preferred to follow this discreet example rather than realize that Goethe was here speaking in a mood that would have been described by Kanzler von Müller as 'negierend, ironisch, widersprechend'.[1]

We cannot read even this reply to Eckermann to the end and naïvely believe that Goethe is still, in 1827, content to hold that 'Gefühl ist alles!' He confesses to having rounded and fully formed, in an artistic manner, not only 'Eindrücke' but also 'Anschauungen'. He had sought 'durch eine lebendige Darstellung (diese) so zum Vorschein zu bringen, dass andere dieselbigen Eindrücke erhielten, wenn sie mein Dargestelltes hörten oder lasen'. He might well have approved of the modern distinction between 'Geist' and 'Seele', but if Eckermann had dared to reply to his final phrase, 'Glauben Herr Geheimrat wirklich, *Faust* wäre ein noch besseres Gedicht gewesen, wenn es für den Verstand durchaus unfasslich ausgefallen wäre?' could his Olympian master have suppressed Olympian laughter?

We know, however, through Houben, Petersen, and others that Eckermann's *Gespräche* do not reveal all that Goethe said to him even about *Faust*. Notably for personal reasons he appears to have suppressed what Petersen[2] describes as 'eine tiefe Erklärung seiner Faustidee und der Bedeutung des Homunkulus als gestaltsuchender Entelechie'. In his Journal Eckermann noted (under date 6 January, 1830), 'Gespräche über den Homunkulus. Entelechie und Unsterblichkeit.' The remarks attributed to Goethe in the 'Gespräche' as made on 4 February, 1829 are clearly closely connected with the entry

---

[1] Julius Petersen, *Die Entstehung der Eckermannschen Gespräche und ihre Glaubwürdigkeit* (Frankfurt a. M.,[2] 1925, p. 152).

[2] *Op. cit.*, p. 49 (cf. Houben's *Eckermann*, p. 448).

in the Journal for 6 January, 1830, even if not predated. They lay stress upon Goethe's belief in 'unsre Fortdauer'. This conviction, Goethe is alleged to have said, 'entspringt mir aus dem Begriff der Tätigkeit'. But this conception of (valid) 'Tätigkeit' is part of Goethe's compound of Greco-Leibnizian *Weltanschauung*. The *harmonia universalis* in which Goethe, like Leibniz, believed is not something 'given', and accepted passively by either reason or feeling, but remains always, as Mahnke[1] observes, an unending 'Aufgabe', to the fulfilment of which 'der schaffende Wille die ganze Kraft seiner Aktivität setzen muss'. And this ethical ideal is essentially a rational ideal, not merely intelligible, but even proper to be taught, *pedagogic*, as Gerland insists.

On the other hand, but equally removed from the 'irrational' element which at times appears in *Faust*, there is in Goethe's poem a perhaps more than Leibnizian insistence upon not only the goodness (or perfection) of God (compared with whom the man-monad is moved only by a 'dunklem Drang'), but upon the 'Liebe von oben', which cannot be conceived of as a mere decorative contrast to the 'strebend sich bemühen', which, as it were, is the price man pays for the right to be 'erlöst'. 'Es irrt der Mensch, so lang er strebt.' But the 'Streben', too, is in the sight of his Creator, who does not hate even the Devil and his like, and whose love surrounds and supports 'die echten Göttersöhne'. This love is clearly extended to Faust, though he does not seem even at the end of the play to be held fit, without further 'Streben' and purification, to see God face to face. He is joined first to the 'bewegte Schar Seliger Knaben', but it was to these that the Pater Seraphicus had said

> Steigt hinan zu höherm Kreise,
> Wachset immer unvermerkt,
> Wie, nach ewig reiner Weise,
> Gottes Gegenwart verstärkt.

[1] *Op. cit.*, p. 70.

Denn das ist der Geister Nahrung,
Die im freiesten Äther waltet,
Ewigen Liebens Offenbarung,
Die zur Seligkeit entfaltet. (II. v, 11918 f.)

It seems undeniable, the poem *as a whole* rests upon a
religious fundament of a definite theological type. Its corner-
stones are the *Prolog im Himmel* and the *Bergschluchten*-scenes
of the Final Act of the Second Part. Its theology is Hebrew-
Rabbinic - Scholastic - Leibnizian, with contributions from
other sources, especially Plotinus and Spinoza. But on the
whole, the medieval concept of God prevails and underlies
all, as in the Gothic sculpture. Faust's 'Tätigkeit' and
'Streben' would be meaningless if the ruler of the world were
not its all-wise Creator and Preserver, the Father of the
'Göttersöhne', who knows Faust to be 'der gute Mensch' and
is ready to designate him to Mephistopheles as 'meinen
Knecht'. Goethe's 'Weltbild' is perhaps most clearly painted
in the *Prolog im Himmel*, but as Rickert says[1] it can 'weder
antik-mittelalterlich noch modern-kopernikanisch zu Ende
gedacht werden'. The Prologue, he adds, cannot be fully
understood, astronomically, without recourse to Pytha-
gorean conceptions. It is more important for us to realize
that it cannot be understood at all without accepting the
fundamental thesis of an all-ruling God, who does not differ
in essentials from the God envisaged by the authors of the
Book of Job, the *Summa theologica*, the medieval Mysteries and
the *Théodicée*. Goethe does not, as some have maintained,
adopt a purely monistic attitude, he makes no pretence that
evil does not exist. *Faust* is perhaps the most famous example
of the struggle between good and evil, but for Faust himself
Goethe does weight the scales. He lets us see from the beginning that God, who is *ex hypothesi* wiser than all the evil
spirits together, has no fear of regretting his 'pact' with
Mephistopheles. This, as I have suggested elsewhere, some-

---

[1] In *Logos*, XIV (1925), p. 15 (*Die Einheit des Faustischen Charakters*).

what detracts from the 'dramatic tension' of the poem,
which some prefer to call an epic, but it is absolutely essential to the plan of the work. The first great 'unity' of *Faust*
is the unity of its theological foundation. The poet's conception of God is the rock upon which the poem is built.

The second great unity of the poem is found in the character of Faust himself. Heinrich Rickert says,[1] 'Die Persönlichkeit seines Helden muss der Dichter vor allem einheitlich
gewollt haben, denn sonst wäre überhaupt keine Einheit des
Ganzen ihm als möglich erschienen.' We have seen that
there is a still more fundamental unity in the concept of God,
but in the drama of the poem the character of Faust himself
is more obviously vital. Faust being a mortal and earth-born
is, in part at least, also earth-bound. His more visible unity,
or rather, as Rickert well says, his *identity* consists precisely in
the struggle in his breast of the 'zwei Seelen', which occupy
it. His higher unity, however, might equally well be said to
consist precisely in the fact that he remains 'der gute
Mensch', however much he fails to 'keep his soul unspotted
from the world'. This 'goodness' appears also to be progres-
sive in that, after the consummation of the Gretchen-tragedy,
his desires seem to take on increasingly a less sensual and
more aesthetic, even finally a more social, aspect. The 'spirit
of darkness' is gradually beaten back by the 'spirit of light'.
He is not a mere average man, but greater by far than most,
and readier than most to swing back towards the true pole,
however far, for a time, the magnet, be it Gretchen,
or even Helena, may have drawn him, trembling, away.
Faust is at once a symbol of humanity and an 'eigenartiges
Individuum' of peculiar grandeur,[2] an 'aussergewöhnlich
grosser Mensch', even an 'Übermensch' in the best sense of

---

[1] Rickert, who has recently treated this 'unity' most fully and ably, does not
seem to do complete justice to the theological unity in the phrase here cited
(from *Logos*, XIV, p. 11), but is otherwise a most admirable guide.
[2] Rickert, *ibid.*, p. 19. See also *ibid.*, p. 36 on 'ich mehr als Cherub' and
Faust's 'übermenschlichen Drang nach Leben und Handeln'.

that rather doubtful term.  His 'goodness', however, is not
effortless like that of the 'schöne Seele'; it can only work
itself out through passionate longing, activity, despair, repentance, hope, renewed activity, strange adventures, care, and
death.  Of Faust's spirit, as of God's creation (Nature), one
may say

> Es wechselt Paradieseshelle
> Mit tiefer schauervoller Nacht.

He is all-compact of contradictory energies.  His grim con-
tract with Mephistopheles emanates from weariness and
despair, yet envisages an endless series of moments of delight.
He is the very symbol of man's unceasing pursuit of an ideal
happiness, yet so conscious of his own unsatisfiable nature
this side of unity with the Divine that he makes his ability
to demand with genuine longing more than Mephistopheles
is able to supply the simple, yet all-sufficing, charm which
sets him free to walk all the precipices of life without fear-
ing spiritual destruction.  Mephistopheles may boast truly
enough

> Staub soll er fressen, und mit Lust,

Faust remains true to his original ideal,

> Dass ich erkenne, was die Welt
> Im Innersten zusammenhält . . .

But also, in spite of all his 'Irren', he makes good his original
boast

> Ich fühle Mut, mich in die Welt zu wagen,
> Der Erde Weh, der Erde Glück zu tragen,
> Mit Stürmen mich herumzuschlagen
> Und in des Schiffbruchs Knirschen nicht zu zagen.

'Geniessen' and 'Erkennen' are the two aims of his existence
and each is valueless without the other.[1]

---

[1] 'Er will die unendliche Natur nicht allein erkennend in Ruhe betrachten,
sondern sie "fassen".  Dieser Ausdruck bedeutet im Gegensatz zu Schauen ein
unmittelbareres Ergreifen, als es durch Erkenntnis möglich ist, ein "Einwirken
in die ganze Natur".  Die Quellen des unmittelbaren Lebens sind es, nach

The idea of 'Streben', the *Leitmotiv* of Faust's character, is equally characteristic of the work of art in which he is used as a symbol. Goethe's *Faust* is, in spite of certain naturalistic scenes, not a realistic work in the common meaning of that term. Neither is Goethe's method 'objective' in the narrow sense often attached to this adjective. As Faust strives towards his new ideal of life, so Goethe strives towards his new ideal of art—more consciously, of course, in the later portions of his poem—and rises up to a conception of art which resembles that which has been discovered in the pictures of Giotto, 'die des autonomen Kunstwerkes', to borrow Dvořák's formula.[1] Though he seems to have begun his work in a considerably more naturalistic mood, we recognize, when we look at it as a whole, a growing tendency towards 'einen heroischen Idealstil . . ., der vielfach mit Bewusstsein von erschöpfender Naturtreue abgewichen ist'. In shaping his material Goethe adopts towards it an independent attitude, in which the will and judgement of the artist are recognized by himself to have an artistic validity transcending that imposed by 'natural' objects and happenings. In the course of *Faust* Goethe passes through all the stages from the almost naïve naturalism of the 'full' Gothic to the much more self-conscious attitude of the great Florentine and his followers.

The parallel should indeed not be pressed too far. Giotto, after all, belongs to the Pre-Renaissance, Goethe to the Post-Baroque era; Giotto was essentially a painter, Goethe above all a poet, though with a good share of the painter's eye. They seem to approach each other most closely in what Dvořák has called[2] 'eine neue künstlerische mit der Wirklichkeit nur lose zusammenhängende Tatsächlichkeit und Überzeugungskraft'.

'Wie ein Zauberspiel' he continues of Giotto, but the words,

denen Faust sich sehnt.' Rickert, *ibid.*, p. 25; cf. pp. 26–9, 31, 35 f., and 41 f. (the suicide-motive itself 'arises in a new hope of happiness and satisfaction of the superhuman urge to activity'). Cf. also pp. 47–52 ('Die zwei Seelen').
[1] Cf. Dvořák, *op. cit.*, p. 219 f.
[2] *Ibid.*, pp. 222–3.

with one little change, would also apply to Goethe in *Faust*, 'musste es den Zeitgenossen erscheinen, als der grosse Künstler an der Hand der alten heiligen Erzählungen vor ihren Augen ein Sein und Geschehen entrollte, in dem aus dem Rohstoff der sinnlichen Erfahrung Formen und Zusammenhänge geschaffen wurden, die den Zufälligkeiten der alltäglichen Wirklichkeit gegenüber als die Offenbarung ungeahnter typischer Wahrheiten und Beziehungen, die der sinnlichen Anschauung zugrunde liegen, erscheinen mussten und die es ermöglichten, die Erzählung in die Sphäre einer eindringlicheren und klareren Wiedergabe der in der Natur waltenden formalen Kräfte und ihrer ursächlichen Verbindungsnormen zu übertragen.'

But Goethe resembles his creature Faust in that he consistently refused to stand still, except in so far as it was necessary in order to secure his foothold before the next step; in fact he followed steadfastly the technique of the experienced mountain-climber. What binds his activities together and at the same time proves his kinship with the Gothic artists is his unfailing consciousness of eternity in the midst of active, but limited, human life. 'Das Bewusstsein der Ewigkeit', Herr Emrich well says in his penetrating study of Goethe's mind,[1] 'ist bei Goethe ein kontinuierlich, durch alle Etappen seines Daseins bewahrtes, und so in einem höheren Sinne für dieses Dasein und seine Deutung konstitutiv'. On the other hand, in Weimar, in Italy, and after his return to Weimar, he opened his mind to experiences which went far beyond and even in some degree contrary to those of his early life. Even in it he had done homage to Shakespeare and Pindar as well as to Erwin von Steinbach; later he drew into his sphere of interest more and more of Greece, Rome, and the Renaissance, without abandoning or unconsciously sloughing this 'Bewusstsein der Ewigkeit'. Thus we find him exhibiting a wider range than Giotto's

---

[1] Hermann Emrich, *Goethes Intuition* (Heidelberger Abhandlungen z. Philos. und ihrer Gesch., hsg. von E. Hoffmann und H. Rickert, No. 14, Tübingen, 1928), p. 17 (with important citations from Goethe).

and compensating thereby for a certain falling-off in dramatic intensity of feeling. 'Das Dämonische' in him is not destroyed, but is kept more firmly in hand, the *eternal values* of 'Standhaftigkeit und Treue in dem gegenwärtigen Zustande' impress themselves upon him. 'Die Tat ist alles'; but 'Tätigkeit' must be regulated. 'Es ist nichts schrecklicher als eine tätige Unwissenheit'[1] becomes a favourite doctrine with Goethe. And in the sphere of art he learns to value highly 'tiefes Nachdenken und ernstes, zusammenfassendes Kunstgefühl'.[2]

It would be childish to expect *Faust* to exhibit uniformity in all its parts. There is hardly any Gothic cathedral which does so; even the great North tower of Erwin's Strassburg 'Münster' does not carry out his original design, and other parts are Romanic. But if we desire to find the nearest analogue to *Faust* in architecture, and it is here rather than in painting that we must seek it, then the building which most forcibly presents itself to our searching gaze is that one south of the Alps, in the Italy to which Goethe fled from Weimar and from which he came back with a new conception of all that is meant by 'art'. Santa Maria del Fiore at Florence is perhaps the grandest example in architecture of the completion of a Gothic edifice of great promise by a master-builder of the early Renaissance working under the inspiration of Rome and Greece and with an immense personal fund of energy, thought, and experience. Goethe himself is not too enthusiastic in the remarks he makes on Brunelleschi,[3]

---

[1] *Maximen und Reflexionen*, ed. M. Hecker, No. 367 (*Jub. Ausg.* Bd. 4, p. 223).

[2] B. Cellini, Anhang zur Lebensbeschreibung (*Jub. Ausg.* Bd. 32, p. 261). This corresponds to his deepening 'Bildungstrieb'. 'Nur gestaltendes Wirken, nicht blosse Beschäftigung, konnte ihn befriedigen', said Henry Thode in one of the best of the older 'Festvorträge' of the Goethe-Gesellschaft at Weimar. See his *Goethe der Bildner* (Heidelberg, 1906), p. 17 and *passim*.

[3] See *Jub. Ausg.* Bd. 32 (*Cellini*, ii), p. 224; but cf. *ibid.*, p. 260, where Goethe names him among 'die trefflichsten florentinischen Bildhauer und Baumeister'. W. von Oettingen's note (*ibid.*, p. 324) on Goethe's expression 'technische Raserei' implies that Ghiberti is the real culprit and 'die virtuose Behandlung der perspektivischen Vertiefung im Relief' what Goethe objects to. He is dealing with 'Bildhauerkunst', not architecture.

and we are assured that the poet's mind did not work on mathematical lines. Yet it is perhaps not too fanciful to see in Giotto's glorious heavenward-pointing tower a counterpart of the *Prolog im Himmel*, and in Brunelleschi's magnificent dome, conditioned as it was, but not spoilt, by the octagonal substructure of his predecessors, a symbol of the Second Part of *Faust*. 'La quale opera quanto sia bella, ella medesima ne fa fede', says Vasari.[1] The fifth act of *Faust* II might be compared to Brunelleschi's lantern-tower that crowns the whole. In graceful lightness it renews the *motif* of the Gothic 'Streben' towards Heaven. After the inward-moving centre-seeking dome has seemed to concentrate the spirit upon the balance of opposing forces rooted in the earth, it lifts the eye suddenly upward and crowns all with the cross, which for the European has become at once the symbol of suffering and the promise of salvation. Faust carries his own cross, but in his unending search for the ideal he is upheld by a Spirit greater than himself, whose dwelling is above and beyond as well as on the earth. The earthly bliss and fruit even of Helena and Faust are doomed to destruction. They chant together

> Der Freude folgt sogleich
> Grimmige Pein. (II. 9901.)

Even Lynceus, whom the world delights, must confess

> Nicht allein mich zu ergetzen,
> Bin ich hier so hoch gestellt:
> Welch ein greuliches Entsetzen
> Droht mir aus der finstren Welt! (II. 11304.)

Faust, too old for enjoyment, learns to know 'die Sorge', goes blind and dies, but 'die ewige Liebe' is proclaimed at

---

[1] 'How beautiful this building is, it will itself bear testimony' (Mrs. Foster's translation). The point has, of course, been disputed. See E. G. Gardner, *The Story of Florence* (London, 1900), p. 266. I am glad to be able to agree honestly with Vasari and Michelangelo rather than with Fergusson.

the last; the angels and 'die seligen Knaben' promise what
Faust has sought from the beginning:

> Göttlich belehret
> Dürft ihr vertraun,
> Den ihr verehret,
> Werdet ihr schaun. (II. 11930.)

The lantern-tower of 'heilige Poesie' points ever upward
towards the face of Almighty God, who is Eternal Love:

> Uns bleibt ein Erdenrest
> Zu tragen peinlich,
> Und wär' er von Asbest,
> Er ist nicht reinlich.
> Wenn starke Geisteskraft
> Die Elemente
> An sich herangerafft,
> Kein Engel trennte
> Geeinte Zwienatur
> Der innigen beiden,
> Die ewige Liebe nur
> Vermag's zu scheiden. (II. 11954 f.)

## BIBLIOGRAPHICAL NOTE

The reader may possibly feel that he has been offered only 'a
distant view' of Goethe's masterpiece. This for the present fulfils
the writer's purpose. Some day he will perhaps undertake a
study of the several parts of *Faust*. Meanwhile he must content himself with having pointed out some illuminating German
literature of recent date. The most convenient and helpful
German editions are those of Professor Robert Petsch (Leipzig,
Bibliographisches Institut), Professor Georg Witkowski (Leipzig,
Max Hesse's Verlag), and the late Professor Erich Schmidt
(vols. 13 and 14 of Cotta's Jubiläumsausgabe). Hermann Bahr's
'Goethebild' (in *Sendung des Künstlers*, Leipzig, 1923) is stimulating
and sanely critical in regard to the works of Hume Brown,
Ludwig, and Gundolf. Professor H. A. Korff's *Geist der Goethezeit*,
II. Teil: *Klassik*, erstes Buch, *Weltanschauung* (issued separately

in 1927) is important. A select list of useful literature is given by Professor J. G. Robertson in his volume on Goethe in Routledge's 'Republic of Letters' (London, 1927). The best English study of *Faust* is probably that of Miss F. Melian Stawell and Mr. G. Lowes Dickinson, *Goethe and Faust, An Interpretation, with passages newly translated into English Verse* (London, G. Bell & Sons, Ltd., 1928). Their 'select bibliography' is far from adequate. It may be supplemented by the up-to-date 'Literaturverzeichnis' in Emrich's monograph *Goethes Intuition* (Tübingen, 1928), an important critical essay written under Rickert's influence. Theodor Däubler's *Sparta* (Leipzig, 1923) is largely occupied with *Faust* II, but will remain 'caviare to the general'. Ernst Maass's work *Goethe und die Antike* (Berlin, 1912) is likely to prove more helpful to most readers and should be better known among us than it is. See especially pp. 315–21 for the close connexion of Helena with Goethe's early works. *Die Ernte* (Halle, 1926), the 'Festschrift' for Franz Muncker edited by Fritz Strich and H. H. Borcherdt, contains articles on *Goethes Weltanschauung im Faust* (by R. Woerner) and *Fausts Himmelfahrt* (by W. Hertz), which supplement those of Burdach and Rickert. Miss Anna Swanwick's English version of both parts (Bohn's Library), with revised Introduction and Bibliography by Professor Karl Breul, has been recently reissued. Professor W. H. van der Smissen's *Goethe's Faust done into English Verse in the Original Metres with Commentary and Notes* (London and Toronto, 1926) is a gallant attempt to provide a '*Faust* for English Readers'. Vol. CXXXV of 'The World's Classics', published by the Oxford University Press, contains Marlowe's *Faustus* and Goethe's *Faust, Part I*, translated by John Anster, with an Introduction by Sir Adolphus Ward.

## II

## THE FIRST ENGLISH VERSIONS OF *FAUST*
## (PART I) AND *DICHTUNG UND WAHRHEIT*[1]

THE years 1922–5 are all centenary years in the history of English translations from Goethe. In 1822 Shelley made his well-known fragmentary versions from *Faust*; they appeared in the first number of *The Liberal* soon after the poet's death. The following year Lord Francis Leveson Gower published *Faust: A Drama by Goethe*, through the house of John Murray, and in 1825 this work 'with [other] translations from the German', reappeared in a second edition, a fact which is not usually mentioned by the historians. A copy of this edition is in my possession, and it is from it that I make my citations. In the meanwhile had appeared another interesting book, which has met with even harder treatment than was meted out to Gower's *Faust*. This was announced as follows in *The Observer* of June 6, 1824, as readers of that valuable weekly were reminded in 1924:

In two vols. 8vo. with a fine portrait, 24*s*. MEMOIRS of GOETHE, author of 'WERTER', 'LEONORA', 'FAUST', etc., written by HIMSELF.—'Goethe has justly been classed by the critics of Germany with the master minds of modern Europe—with Shakespeare, with Dante, and with Cervantes, not as possessing powers of a similar kind, but as enjoying, like those great men, the reputation of being, beyond all comparison, the first of his age and country'. Published and sold by H. Colburn, 8 New Burlington-street.

Shelley's Fragments from *Faust* are too well known to need further comment, except in so far as they may have influenced Gower in one point to which I shall revert. Gower's *Faust* is more interesting than the *Memoirs*, but a brief notice of the latter may be given before we discuss the *Faust*. In

[1] Read before the English Goethe Society at a meeting held at King's College, University of London, on March 17, 1926. The title is without prejudice to the claims of the abbreviated prose version which accompanied the *Outlines* of Retzsch, published in London in 1820.

regard to both works, I shall attempt, not exactly a 'Rettung', but at least a more historical and impartial account of these translations than seems hitherto to have been thought necessary.

## I. The 'Memoirs'

The actual title ran thus: '*Memoirs of Goëthe: written by himself*'. The work is in two large octavo volumes, well printed, with wide margins, by S. and R. Bentley for the publisher, Henry Colburn, who specialized in autobiographical works (e.g. the Diaries of Pepys and Evelyn) as well as in popular novels, such as those of Lady Morgan and Theodore Hook, and also deserves respect as the founder of the *Literary Gazette*, 'upon the plan of a popular German prototype', as Henry Curwen remarks in his *History of Booksellers*. The translator is not named upon the title-page or elsewhere, and, so far as I know, his identity remains in doubt. Conjecture on this matter is at present purely speculative, although if Henry Colburn's business books have survived, and could be consulted, the problem might be solved. In the meantime one might hazard a guess that H. E. Lloyd, the clerk in the Foreign Department of the Post Office, described by Curwen as 'a good linguist, and a well-known translator from the German', and by Jerdan (*Autobiography*, iii, p. 236) as 'my indefatigable coadjutor for many a year', and contributor to the *Literary Gazette* (in 1818), of 'an original translation of the Remarks of the Austrian Arch-dukes' (John and Lewis) tour in England', is likely to have had some hand in the matter. But others, for example Miss Ross, daughter of William Ross of *The Times*, also occur to one as possible translators, and the matter must be left in obscurity. An appeal to Colburn's successors, Messrs. Hurst and Blackett, has elicited a courteous reply but no information on this point. As the translator writes of the 'minister' of Sesenheim, he may have been a Nonconformist.

The translation, as most of those who have mentioned it say or imply, is certainly far from being adequate according to modern standards. Nor were the contemporary critics pleased with it. The attack on Colburn and his hack, if such he was, was ably led by a writer in the *Westminster Review* for April 1824 (vol. i, no. 2), who had no difficulty in pointing out a variety of drawbacks and serious faults, but also at times over-reached himself in his desire to castigate 'the translator's entire ignorance', as he puts it, 'not of the German language merely, but of the history, customs, and institutions of the country'. This critic's captiousness comes out pretty clearly when he falls foul of the translator for rendering the term *Repetent* by 'private tutor', and '*Hefte,* that is the MS. notes of the lectures', as 'a book'! For myself, I can only say that the word 'tutor' (i.e. in a particular subject, as it is most often used now at Oxford) is best rendered by this very word 'Repetent', but doubtless to the reviewer 'private tutor' suggested more the idea of 'Hofmeister'. Many other errors noted are less venial, but in dealing with one of them (from Book xiii, *Memoirs* ii, p. 42) the reviewer misquotes the translator, making him speak of persons who are 'led astray by excessive desire', instead of 'led astray by extravagant desires'. The phrase, it is true, does not give Goethe's meaning, but such a keen reviewer should at least have cited more accurately the words he condemns.

In point of fact the English translator was here, as in some other places, following too carefully the French version, upon which, as the reviewer rightly guessed, the *Memoirs* are largely based. One has to say 'guessed', for the reviewer himself betrays the fact that he did not take the trouble to refer to the French *Mémoires.* He remarks, in objecting to the rendering 'the book of Facetiæ', that 'the French translator . . . *would be very likely* to write "livre de faceties" ' (*sic*), but fails to verify this, and he goes out of his way to correct the title, 'Quatre fils Aimon', to 'Quatre fils *d'* Aimon', being himself oblivious of the fact that the English translator faithfully reproduces here the consecrated French form. Moreover, it was probably not an accident that the French title of what was originally a French *conte bleu* was here retained in the English translation.

Very few of those who mention Aubert de Vitry's *Mémoires de Goëthe* (2 vols., octavo, Paris, 1823), seem to have compared it carefully with the English translation, and I, too, have had to rely upon a brief collation made in a few hours at the British Museum, as I could not find a copy in Oxford. But F. Baldensperger and those who follow him are clearly correct in holding that the English translation derives directly from de Vitry rather than from *Aus meinem Leben*, 'the original publication from which', the Preface of the *Memoirs* tells us with some lack of candour, 'the following translation is executed'. One may suppose that *Dichtung und Wahrheit* was on the translator's desk, but his eyes seem to have been mainly upon the *Mémoires*.

His very title betrays him, for, the word *Memoirs* apart, he has faithfully reproduced the spelling Goëthe, which called forth the scorn of the *Westminster* reviewer, who, however, fails to buttress his statement that 'this book must have been translated from the French' by citing the title of de Vitry's work. He may have been caused to hesitate by knowing that in France the spelling 'Goète' was also used. Baldensperger, in *Goethe en France*, p. 113, has a quotation from the *Muse française* (of 1823) regarding 'les poésies . . . de *Goète* et de Schiller, qui ont obtenu tant de succès en Allemagne'. The pronunciation was, of course, dissyllabic (go-et), and a similar error used, I fancy, to be current in England among the less instructed. English historians may still be found who talk of Metternitch, and Victor Yugo, or Hewgo, seems to be almost ineradicable even in our seats of learning.

Again there is the length, or rather the shortness, of the English translation, upon which the *Westminster* also commented severely. It does not, in fact, contain quite three-fourths of the original. But it has, in the text, on a rough calculation, about 9,000 more words than de Vitry used, although not including all his matter. I omit, of course, the *Voyage en Italie* (the third part of de Vitry's work), as this does not appear in the English translation, and it may be added that the biographical notices at the end are briefer in the latter. The account of Goethe in the *Postscript* to vol. ii of the English translation (pp. 161–74, *not* 179, as Carré in his *Bibliographie*, p. 92, states) incorporates much of de Vitry's 'Introduction', but is at times better informed or better arranged chronologically. It also mentions the title of 'Joerden's Lexicon of German Authors', which is withheld by de Vitry in citing Heinse's letter to Gleim ('Nous avons Goëthe avec nous: c'est un beau jeune homme de vingt-cinq ans' . . .).

The *Memoirs of Goëthe*, then, is not exactly an 'original' translation, and justice in the main rests with the *Westminster* reviewer. But his views have been quoted a little too freely, even, it would seem, by Carlyle himself. In the *Miscellaneous Essays*, vol. i, there are two notes on the *Memoirs*. In the note on Goethe, from *German Romance* (1827), he is 'sorry to understand that the English version of the work is not from the German, but from the French', judges 'by the size of the book' (as described by the reviewer?) the amount of curtailment, and deprecates, without pointing out, 'additions, which *probably* are still more offensive'. In the essay on Goethe, of 1828 (*Foreign Review*, No. 3), he also warns his readers against the *Memoirs* as the work of 'that German translator, whom *indignant Reviewers* have proved to know *no* German'. [My italics, except for *no* and the title.] But he has a twinge of conscience now, and adds 'But the unhappy Dragoman has already been chastised, perhaps too sharply. If, warring with the reefs and breakers and cross eddies of life, he still hover on this side the shadow of Night, and any word of ours might reach him, we would rather say: Courage, Brother! grow honest and times will mend.' Had Carlyle, in the meantime, looked into the *Memoirs* and been surprised, like the present writer, to find them somewhat better than their reputation?

For, with all their faults, these volumes are based on good French, and render it pretty accurately. It is customary to cite Goethe's application to de Vitry of that somewhat overworked Italian proverb, 'traduttore traditore'. A fuller and more favourable view of de Vitry's work is to be found in the draft of Goethe's letter to the translator (Weimar, den 29. März 1824; *Briefe*, Weimarer Ausg., xxxviii. pp. 96–7), in which we read the words:

> Jeder Autor muss wissen was er seiner Nation, unter gewissen Umständen und Bedingungen mittheilen kann, der französische ist hierin beschränkter als der deutsche und muss, wenn er zu übersetzen unternimmt, eigentlich immer umbilden; es ist mir diess von jeher bekannt und es durfte mich nicht wundern dass meine Arbeiten auf solche Weise behandelt wurden.

It is significant that Goethe adds: 'Erhalten Sie mir Ihre Neigung und beachten meine Sicilianische Reise, den Feldzug von 1792 und was etwa in der Folge sich hier anschliessen möge.' These are strange words to come from any man to his betrayer! This French version was, after all, a good deal better than none at all, and, as Baldensperger remarks (*op. cit.*, p. 269), it was pretty well received, although the public was not really ripe for it.

Much the same might be said of the English version. It was as good or better than could be hoped for at a time when even the *Westminster* reviewer thought it proper to remark that 'with the exception of the Elective Affinities ... we know none of the author's works so little fitted for translation'. If England received at first an inadequate version of *Dichtung und Wahrheit*, the English were themselves to blame.

Finally, to show that the work, however imperfect, was

not without its own charm, nor, generally, in bad style, let me cite the version given of the famous account of *Laocoon* (vol. i, pp. 236 f.):

> With what joy did we hail this luminous ray, which a thinker of the first order suddenly struck out from clouds of darkness! All the fire of youth would be requisite to conceive the effect which Lessing's Laocoon produced upon us, when the work first drew us out of the regions of barren contemplation, to launch us into the free and fertile field of thought. The long misunderstood adage of 'Ut pictura poësis' was at length elucidated. The difference between the art of painting and that of writing was at length rendered obvious. It was seen that, although the bases of these arts might touch each other, their summits were distinct and separate. In fact, it is in vain that the painter envies the poet the faculty of seizing and characterizing all objects, and of overstepping the limits of the beautiful: these limits will nevertheless remain the line of demarcation which painting cannot pass; for its object is to satisfy the eye, which nothing but the beautiful can delight. The poet, on the contrary, labours for the imagination; which, although it repels odious objects themselves, does not object to their representation. A single glance, like a flash of lightning, revealed to us all the consequences of this magnificent thought. All the superannuated criticism, which had formerly been the only guide of our judgments and reflections, was now thrown aside like a worn-out garment. Delivered from these trammels, we looked with an eye of compassion on the pictures and poetry of the sixteenth century, in which life, death, and the evils which necessity or chance inflict on the world, were represented under the most ridiculous forms.

The end, of course, is here very weak, and the omissions after it are, no doubt, very serious. But it cannot truthfully be said, as was said in the *Westminster Review*, that 'nearly all the most significant and pregnant passages' were omitted from the book. On the whole, it was much better than nothing, and one feels sure that it must have interested a large number of readers who would never have read a single page of the original German.

## II. *Leveson Gower's Version of 'Faust' (Part I)*

Lord Francis Leveson Gower's work appeared under his own name—he only became Earl of Ellesmere in 1846—and I give this as it stands on the title-page of the second edition of the book (London, John Murray, 1825). This edition is in two pretty little duodecimo volumes, the second of which is mainly filled out with the lyrical 'Translations from the German'. The latter include: *The Song of the Bell, The Partition of the Earth, To Minna, The Ideal, The Feast of Victory, The Veiled Statue at Sais, Epithalamium, Honour to Woman, The Gods of Greece*, all of these following the half-title 'Translations from Schiller'. The other poems translated are (the) *Lay of the Imprisoned Knight* (the title being followed by the name of GOËTHE, spelt as in the anonymous *Memoirs*), *War Song of the New Zealander* (BÜRGER), *The Grave* (by SALIS), *War Song* (THEODORE KÖRNER), *War Song written before the Battle of Danneberg*, and *Song of the Sword* (written a few hours before the death of the author in battle: KÖRNER). *Faust* occupies 279 pages in all, the lines being widely spaced, about 20 on a page, including the names of the actors. '*Lessing's Faust*', with a brief note citing Mme de Staël (the spelling of Goethe's name being Göethe this time) [1] as well as Engel's account of the work, is rendered, of course in prose, on pp. 79–85 of vol. ii.

There is no need to dwell upon these minor efforts of Gower's here, but it may be of interest, before we turn to *Faust*, to cite a contemporary criticism of them, as previously issued in 1824, along with some 'Original Poems', which, the writer cruelly remarks at the end, 'will not engage the attention of any reader beyond the circle of the noble author's personal connexions'. The review, which chances to stand at the end of the same number of the *Westminster* that condemns

---

[1] So also on p. 1 of vol. i ('Lines which precede the Prologue to Faustus. Göethe.').

the *Memoirs*, begins, however, with the translations and finds their matter, at least, of value.

Till within a few years (it observes), Wieland's Oberon, by Mr. Sotheby, and Göthe's Iphigenia, Lessing's Nathan the Wise, and Bürger's Leonora, and other ballads, by Mr. Taylor, of Norwich, constituted the whole body of poetical translation from the German. Mr. Beresford's German Erato, though of very moderate execution, introduced to the English reader a number of lyrical pieces set to music. But, within a short period, German literature has become a study among our younger poets, and a copious anthology might already be collected from the versions which have recently appeared in our popular magazines. The present publication is a respectable addition to our stock of poetical translation, though we cannot class our author with Gillies or Carey, who have lately carried this elegant art to a high degree of excellence. Lord L. Gower has had the judgment to select compositions which have in their *matter* a claim to public attention, independently of their poetical form. This is particularly true of the poems of Schiller . . . A translator might distrust his power of transferring to a foreign language the exquisite grace, which a perfect mastery of style throws over all the minor poems of Göthe . . . who yet might hope to impart the sterling sense of the significant and weighty lines of Schiller. The Veiled Statue at Sais and the Ideal, are philosophical poems, much better entitled to that character than the popular common-places of the Essay on Man. 'The Gods of Greece' is a polemical ode, which, at its first appearance (like the author's first tragedy, the Robbers) drew down upon him a host of angry adversaries. But it will not be *mistaken* here. The orthodox Johnson at least has sanctioned it by the remark, that the Grecian mythology will always be the religion of poets. Even the Epithalamium has in it more of contemplation than of desire. We make one extract only from 'Honour to Woman,' that our readers may appreciate the translator's effort in copying the metre of the original, to give a male and female character to the verses which respectively characterise the sexes . . .

This notice is not devoid of historical interest. One sees, above all, the kind of non-aesthetic criticism which our translator was liable to meet with. It hardly seems necessary to scrutinize the reviews of his *Faust*. I am content to accept here the account of M. Carré, 'La traduction de lord Gower est saluée avec un enthousiasme exagéré par les conservateurs écossais, sévèrement critiquée par les libéraux londoniens'. But I dissent, in some measure, from his judgement (is it first hand?) of the work of Gower, when he calls it 'sa lâche et médiocre version en vers, travail d'écolier ambitieux qui connaissait à peine l'allemand'. This judgement is, of course, traditional: it contains a measure of truth, but not, I suggest, the whole truth.

'Lâche' means either 'cowardly' or 'loose'. It doubtless refers chiefly to Gower's sins of omission, for, positively, it was surely a bold, almost a rash act, for a young man of twenty-three, practically an undergraduate, to set about turning *Faust*, of all works, into English, and not into prose, but into verse. If the verse, on the whole, smacks more of Thomas Moore than of Byron or Shelley, that is hardly Gower's fault. He may have over-estimated his powers, the word 'ambitieux' may stand; but 'qui connaissait à peine l'allemand' is scarcely quite fair to our poet, even if he had the misfortune to be still an 'écolier'. To vary the monotony of our prose, let us look at his version in a difficult place, in which he is neither very happy nor completely baffled. It may remind us that he ventures on the magnificent opening of the Prologue in Heaven, though he fails, and this is perhaps the head and front of his offence, to give us the interview between Mephistopheles and the Lord, either from timidity or from a real, if misdirected, piety. Here is the 'Song of the three Archangels' as he renders it:

RAPHAEL.

The sun his ancient hymn of wonder
Is pouring out to kindred spheres,
And still pursues, with march of thunder,
His preappointed course of years.

E

Thy visage gives thy angels power,
    Though none its dazzling rays withstand,
And bright, as in their natal hour,
    Creation's dazzling realms expand.

### GABRIEL.

And still the earth's enduring motion
    Revolves with uncomputed speed,
And o'er the chequer'd earth and ocean
    Darkness and light by turns succeed.
The billowy waste of seas is boiling
    From deep primeval rocks below,
Yet on their destined march are toiling
    The rocks that stand, the waves that flow.

### MICHAEL.

The whirlwind and the storm are raging
    From sea to land, from land to main;
And adverse elements engaging,
    The trembling universe enchain.
The lightnings of the dread destroyer
    Precede his thunders through the air;
Yet, at the nod of their employer,
    The servants of his wrath forbear.

### CHORUS.

Thy visage gives thy angels power,
    Though none its dazzling rays withstand,
And bright, as in their natal hour,
    Creation's dazzling realms expand.

Shelley's version of this prelude is on the whole closer to
the original and more poetical, but the difference is not very
striking.  Shelley's Chorus runs:

The Angels draw strength from thy glance,
    Though no one comprehend thee may:—
Thy world's unwithered countenance
    Is bright as on creation's day.

Perhaps Leveson Gower has not all the worst of it here, and, in any case, Shelley had been first on the scene. He had also, of course, been bold enough to give the rest of the Prologue, but then he was already known to the Philistines as 'that damned atheist', and in this direction had little to lose in reputation. Also, he was seven or eight years older than Leveson Gower. It seems a little pompous to be severe about the omission by the latter of this scene, when one finds in the *Edinburgh Review* for July, 1824 (no. lxxx), in a tolerably favourable account of Shelley's fragments from *Faust*, the chorus of Witches dismissed with the words, 'the preter-natural imagery in all this medley, is, we confess, (com-paratively speaking) meagre and monotonous; but there is a squalid nudity, and a fiendish irony and scorn thrown over the whole, that is truly edifying'. Leveson Gower may well have been uncertain whether the dialogue between the Lord and the Devil was sufficiently 'edifying' to be repeated in English so soon. And he may not have cared to rival Shelley's version of the scene.

No one will expect me to go through Gower's rendering scene by scene at this date. Let me end with a couple of quotations from him, and a very brief moral. The first volume closes with this attempt to render 'Meine Ruh' ist hin':

> My peace is vanish'd,
>     My heart is sore:
> I shall find it never,
>     And never more!

> Where he is not,
>     I find my tomb;
> And the sunniest spot
>     Is turn'd to gloom.

> My aching head
>     Will burst with pain—
> And the sense has fled
>     My wilder'd brain.

I look through the glass
  Till my eyes are dim;
The threshold I pass
  Alone for him.

His lofty step,
  And his forehead high,
His winning smile,
  And his beaming eye!

His fond caress,
  So rich in bliss!
His hand to press—
  And ah! his kiss!

My peace is vanish'd—

    \*    \*    \*    \*[1]

Could I but find him,
  My grief were past!
These arms should bind him,
  And hold him fast.

Could I kiss him and cherish,
  As I could kiss!
But thus—and perish
  In doing this!

Not brilliant, indeed, but, sung with due feeling in the
style of 1823, the lines would pass, one feels. Let us next see
what the translator can do with Faust's speech in answer
to Margaret's anxious exclamation, 'Faith, then, you have
none.'[2]

### FAUST

Do not distort my answer, lovely one.
Who could himself compel
To say he disbelieves
The being whose presence all must feel so well?
The All-creator,

[1] The repetition of this verse is, rather unhappily, indicated thus in Gower's text.
[2] vol. ii, pp. 3–4.

The All-sustainer,
Does he not uphold
Thyself, and me, and all?
Does not yon vaulted Heaven expand
Round the fast earth on which we stand?
Do we not hail it, though from far
The light of each eternal star?
Are not my eyes in yours reflected?
And, all these living proofs collected,
Do not they flash upon the brain,
Do not they press upon the heart,
The trace of Nature's mystic reign?
Inhale the feeling till it fill
The breast, then call it what you will.
Call it an influence from above—
Faith, heaven, or happiness, or love,
I have no name by which to call
The secret power—'tis feeling all.

Inadequate, and, alas, inaccurate, but good enough to make a considerable impression on unsophisticated readers not versed in the original. And, above all, an attempt to render *in verse* a great poem, of which no *prose* version could possibly give the true feeling, however much of the contents it conveyed. For, in such works, rhythm and sense are so wedded that they cannot be divorced. Columbus discovered America, but he had no very clear idea of the extent and riches of the continent he discovered. Lord Leveson Gower's conception of the depth and richness of *Faust*, as it appears in his version, leaves much to be desired, but let us remember and honour him as the 'écolier ambitieux' who made the discovery that Goethe's great dramatic poem was worthy of being rendered into our mother tongue, and had the courage to essay the task.[1]

[1] The stirring of the *Zeitgeist* presumably accounts for the fact that the first two French versions also appeared in 1823. (Cf. F. Baldensperger, *Goethe en France*, p. 127.) Moreover Goethe himself was now more friendly towards the Romantics, 'deren Kämpfe in Italien und Frankreich er teilnehmend verfolgte' (Max Koch, *Gesch. der deutschen Lit.*, Leipzig, Göschen, 1911, p. 223).

# III
## FATE AND GUILT IN THE GERMAN DRAMA, 1799–1833.[1]

OUR theme is wide, our time short: I will come as quickly as I can to grips with my subject, which you will not expect me to treat at full length. My aim will rather be to take certain selected works as specimens and seek to bring out the characteristics which relate them to, or distinguish them from, one another. It is clear that almost every play of the higher type, certainly every tragedy worth our attention, might offer us aid in the study of our problem. There is much that I must indicate very cursorily, much that must remain unsaid, much perhaps that will sound theoretical or dogmatic, if you do not bear in mind that brevity, like charity, covers a multitude of sins. I seek to exhibit the typical, the outstanding, from a distance, like a man displaying the Alps through a telescope, not like a geologist examining rocks through a microscope.

The ideas of fate and guilt are evidently 'uralt'. Martin Luther relied on age-long experience when he wrote in the year 1520 the words, 'Wer schuldig ist, der leide! Was geistlich Recht dawider gesagt hat, ist lauter ertichtet römisch Vermessenheit.' 'Whoso is guilty, let him suffer!' It is the very formula of ancient Greek religion and the ancient Greek drama, where it is brought into direct juxtaposition with the concept of fate. Aeschylus puts into the mouth of the Chorus in the *Choephoroi* the most solemn formulation of the law: age-old is the proverb that says, 'Let him that did it suffer':

$$\delta\rho\acute{a}\sigma\alpha\nu\tau\iota \ \pi\alpha\theta\epsilon\hat{\iota}\nu,$$
$$\tau\rho\iota\gamma\acute{\epsilon}\rho\omega\nu \ \mu\hat{\upsilon}\theta\text{os} \ \tau\acute{a}\delta\epsilon \ \phi\omega\nu\epsilon\hat{\iota}.$$

Age-old, indeed, is this cry of man's, and from the beginning he has set it down as the voice of his God. In the book

[1] Read before the English Goethe Society at a meeting in King's College, University of London, on January 27, 1927.

of Genesis (iii. 17) we hear it in the clearest language, 'Because thou hast hearkened unto the voice of thy wife . . . cursed is the ground for thy sake; in sorrow shalt thou eat of it all thy days.' And in the Far East the same belief. In the year 1133 B.C. the Chinese Emperor Wu Wang, speaking to his nobles, represented himself as the co-worker with Heaven in the putting down of crime. 'The iniquity of Shang is full. Heaven gives command to destroy it. If I did not comply with Heaven, my iniquity would be as great.'

But there is a contrasted view. Who shall say when first there arose in man the bitter thought, 'Not only am I not my brother's keeper, nay, I am not even my own. I am not master of my fate, and for the crime I have committed there is none dare blame me. For either I have done what the high gods themselves willed, or else they themselves are subject to some stronger, more mysterious, less kindly Power, to that which has no name but the name of the thing that must befall—necessity, Ananke.' Adam himself, had he dared, would surely have questioned God and said, 'Why didst thou give me a wife to tempt me, Why didst thou permit the serpent to enter the garden of Eden? Thine is the fault, or else there is no fault. Thou and I do but fulfil the law of the Universe.' The Greeks, even the most religious among them, even Aeschylus, did not hesitate at times to formulate as clearly as is possible the last consequences of this argument. Ananke rules Zeus himself. Prometheus cries τέχνη δ' Ἀνάγκης ἀσθενεστέρα μακρῷ (P. V. 510), to which the Chorus duly replies with the question: τίς οὖν Ἀνάγκης ἐστὶν οἰακοστρόφος, who then is the steersman of Necessity? Dr. Wilhelm Gundel,[1] who has dealt with this question in a special inquiry, says, 'Darin ist unter ἀνάγκη die volle Persönlichkeit verstanden, ihre Vollstreckerinnen (οἰακόστροφοι) sind die Moiren und Erinyen, sie steuern das Welten- und Schicksalsschiff, so wie

[1] W. Gundel, *Beiträge zur Entwickelungsgeschichte der Begriffe Ananke und Heimarmene*, Giessen, 1914, p. 28.

es die Gebieterin und Herrin heischt; ihr Wort ist die πεπρω-
μένη (die 'Vorsehung'), der keiner, selbst Zeus nicht, entrinnt,
und deren Sinn starr und unbeugsam ist . . .' This concept is
elaborated and modified by Euripides, the Stoics, and the
Roman dramatist Seneca.

Passing here to German literature, we find in the seven-
teenth century, in Opitz and Gryphius, for example, a
general tone which reminds us of Stoic philosophy or Senecan
drama, but of course now mingled with Christian conceptions of life and death, virtue and vice. But in France the
Abbé Dubos, a contemporary of Gottsched, pronounced in
1719 in his *Réflexions critiques sur la poésie et sur la peinture* (I.1.5)
a fruitful phrase. 'Un Stoicien', he wrote, 'jouerait un rôle
bien ennuieux dans une tragédie.' You, who know your
*Laokoon*, will recall at once the phrase in which Lessing, with
no acknowledgement to Dubos, recasts this idea in his laconic
way: 'Alles Stoische ist untheatralisch'; this idea is one of the
main pillars of Lessing's theory of tragedy.

Consciously or unconsciously, the 'Storm and Stress'
writers adopt this phrase as their motto, and in a few years
the bookshops are full of *Götzen, Werthers, Ugolinos*, and *Räuber*,
none of whom show the least intention of suffering in silence.
But the storm blows over, Goethe and Schiller reach years of
discretion, face the problems of the acted drama, study the
great French and Greek models, make their peace with
society and philosophy, and begin to see life steadily and see
it whole. In *Egmont* we have a characteristic mingling of the
earlier and the maturer outlook, but as in *Faust* the hero of
the last scenes differs notably from him of the first. The
famous picture of the 'Sonnenpferde der Zeit', whipped on
by invisible spirits, hurtling the light chariot of our fate along
the rocky, precipitous track, while we, with a good courage,
can but seek to turn aside the wheels from sheer disaster,
seems to belong to the year 1775. And even here we find
a Stoic note of resignation, a recognition, almost in the vein

of Epictetus, of the 'Allwalten der Notwendigkeit', clad in language which inevitably reminds us of the classical myth of Phaëthon.

A further stage is seen in *Wilhelm Meister*, in some respects Goethe's most baroque work of art, and the only one, I think, in which he indicates his appreciation of the importance of Andreas Gryphius. Here the concept of 'Geleitetwerden' on the whole supersedes that of being run away with. 'Du kommst mir vor, wie Saul, der Sohn Kis, der ging fort, die Eselinnen seines Vaters zu finden und fand ein Königreich'; this quiet picture from the Old Testament deserves at least to be weighed beside the gloomy lines of the Harper:

> Ihr führt ins Leben uns hinein,
> Ihr lasst den Armen schuldig werden,
> Dann überlasst ihr ihn der Pein:
> Denn alle Schuld rächt sich auf Erden.

It cannot be denied that this song and the painful story of the harper were probably not without their effect as models on the writers of the fate-drama, but they do not seem to me to represent, any more than the wonderful *Gesang der Parzen*, Goethe's habitual outlook upon crime and punishment.

Here let us turn for a while to Schiller. In his essay, *Über die tragische Kunst*, 1792, Schiller introduces the idea of *force majeure:*

Unser Mitleid wird nicht weniger geschwächt, wenn der Urheber eines Unglücks, dessen schuldlose Opfer wir bemitleiden sollen, unsre Seele mit Abscheu erfüllt. Es wird jederzeit der höchsten Vollkommenheit seines Werks Abbruch tun, wenn der tragische Dichter nicht ohne einen Bösewicht auskommen kann, und wenn er gezwungen ist, die Grösse des Leidens von der Grösse der Bosheit herzuleiten. Shakespeares Iago und Lady Macbeth, Kleopatra in der Rodogune, Franz Moor in den Räubern zeugen für diese Behauptung.

One sees here how far Schiller is from grasping the true tragic value of such 'criminals' as Lady Macbeth and Cleopatra, besides whom, indeed, Franz Moor is almost a machine. One is, then, not much surprised when he adds:

Ein Dichter, der sich auf seinen wahren Vorteil versteht, wird das Unglück nicht durch einen bösen Willen, der Unglück beabsichtet, noch viel weniger durch einen Mangel des Verstandes, sondern durch den Zwang der Umstände herbeiführen.

We have arrived at 'the force of circumstances', we are perilously near to the concept of 'ineluctable Fate'.

Schiller also here praises Goethe's *Iphigenie* on the ground that Thoas, who might have wrecked the purpose of Orestes and his sister, refrains and chooses to suffer nobly, though himself the victim of circumstances. Still higher is the type of tragedy represented, at its best, by Corneille's *Cid*. But here 'Notwendigkeit' is seen at work and Schiller expresses clearly his view that

eine blinde Unterwürfigkeit unter das Schicksal immer demütigend und kränkend für freie, sich selbst bestimmende Wesen ist. Dies ist es, was uns auch in den vortrefflichsten Stücken der griechischen Bühne etwas zu wünschen übrig lässt, weil in allen diesen Stücken zuletzt an die Notwendigkeit appelliert wird und für unsre vernunftfordernde Vernunft immer ein unaufgelöster Knoten zurück bleibt.

Schiller goes on to claim that the modern tragedian, with the aid of 'einer geläuterten Philosophie', has proved his power to untie this knot. For he possesses 'ein deutliches Bewusstsein einer teleologischen Verknüpfung der Dinge, einer erhabenen Ordnung, eines gütigen Willens'. But here he is perhaps doing some injustice to the Greek view of Ananke and further assuming, with Kant, a teleological theology which Kant himself failed to prove. For the purposes of the dramatist he has advanced no further than Hans Sachs himself and is at the disadvantage of having lost the naïve outlook of the sixteenth century. The belief that it is necessary and possible, 'den einzelnen Misslaut in der grossen Harmonie aufzulösen', is more consoling to the philosopher than helpful to the tragedian, but it is probably this belief which leads, one is inclined to say misleads, Schiller into his quandary when he comes to deal with the case of Wallenstein.

You remember the letter of November 28th, 1796, in which Schiller explains to Goethe 'das Proton Pseudos in der Katastrophe, wodurch sie für eine tragische Entwicklung so ungeschickt ist', a root-difficulty which so far is 'noch nicht ganz überwunden'. 'Das eigentliche Schicksal tut noch zu wenig, und der eigene Fehler des Helden noch zu viel zu seinem Unglück', he complains sadly, and can only restore his courage by an appeal to Shakespeare. 'Mich tröstet hier aber einigermassen das Beispiel des Macbeth, wo das Schicksal ebenfalls weit weniger Schuld hat als der Mensch, dass er zu Grunde geht.' If *Faust* was Goethe's 'Tragelaph', *Wallenstein* was still more obviously Schiller's. He is fascinated by a hero whose character fits so ill with his philosophy that, in order to portray him to his own satisfaction, he feels forced to modify the most obvious cause of his downfall, and endeavour to represent him as a good man in the grip of a cruel Fate rather than as a great man destroyed by a great, perhaps the greatest possible, failing.

The truth seems to be that Schiller did not consider Wallenstein to be a man of genius. The proof of this contention depends on the *argumentum a silentio*, but it is here, I think, convincing. In the essay on *Naive und sentimentalische Dichtung* we have the famous definition of the indispensable quality of genius:

Naiv muss jedes wahre Genie sein, oder es ist keines. Seine Naivetät allein macht es zum Genie, und was es im Intellektuellen und Ästhetischen ist, kann es im Moralischen nicht verleugnen . . .

This is no definition that applies only to poets. Columbus, Archimedes, and Hippocrates are mentioned beside Dante, Cervantes, and Shakespeare, and then, as though to underline the fact, and to give us a clear lead about Wallenstein, Schiller adds

Ja, was noch weit mehr Schwierigkeit zu haben scheint, selbst der grosse Staatsmann und Feldherr werden, sobald sie durch ihr Genie gross sind, einen naiven Charakter zeigen. Ich will hier unter den Alten nur an Epaminondas und Julius Cäsar, unter den Neuern nur an Heinrich IV. von Frankreich, Gustav Adolf von Schweden und den Zar Peter den Grossen erinnern. Der Herzog von Marlborough, Turenne, Vendome zeigen uns alle diesen Charakter.

The effect of the omission of the name of Wallenstein (after that of Gustavus Adolphus) is almost more striking than would be the effect if Schiller had written: 'den Namen des grossen Wallenstein hierher zu setzen, wird wohl niemand wagen'.

So Schiller comes to write his most imposing drama with one hand tied behind his back. The hero he has chosen is neither a genius, nor, properly speaking, a good man, such as Aristotle demanded, with a small defect. He is 'ein ver-wegener Charakter' and 'der unbezähmten Ehrsucht Opfer'. The poet proposes to bring him 'menschlich näher', but not, as we might have hoped, by showing us in him the picture of ourselves—a second *Hamlet*, but by the older method of Greek, or rather Senecan, art:

Sie sieht den Menschen in des Lebens Drang
Und wälzt die grössre Hälfte seiner Schuld
Den unglückseligen Gestirnen zu.

It is a strange spectacle. Schiller, who believes as a philosopher, with Kant, in 'the moral law within us' is here endeavouring to mingle with the human the other world of 'the starry heavens above'. Not content with the clash of human characters and the defeat of reason by desire, he falls back upon the workings of an inscrutable Fate and alleges that he does in obedience to the behest of art something which really proceeds from his distaste for moral weakness and duplicity in the great and nearly heroic. Hence this carefully contrived 'Charakterbild' 'schwankt' in one way 'in der Geschichte', but, in another way, in Schiller's play. In his presentation of his hero we seem to see him at the game of 'he loves me, he loves me not'. As Helene Raff put it some ten years ago, 'nichts Eigentümlicheres, nichts Zwiespältigeres im Grunde als Schillers Stellung zu Wallenstein'.[1] This is because the poet who himself wrote, in that same letter of November 28th, 1796, concerning Wilhelm Meister: 'Er versagt uns die nächste Befriedigung, die wir fordern (die Bestimmtheit)', has himself chosen for his hero a man whose most decided trait is his horror of coming to a final decision upon vital matters. But instead of clearly admitting this to himself and building firmly on it, he attempts, half-heartedly enough, to exhibit him as another Sisera against whom fight the stars in their courses. The marvel is that the play, nevertheless, moves with majesty and vigour towards its appointed goal. Schiller, indeed, would perhaps have said that it does so partly because he had the worldly wisdom to refuse to answer this question of the freedom of the will, which Goethe, who was reading Milton's *Paradise Lost*, raised in a rather drastic manner on July 30, 1799. Schiller's reply, of August 2, appears to be casuistical, it so plainly evades the issue by suggesting that the poet and the orator are not concerned with elemental truths:

Gottlob, dass wir nicht berufen sind, das Menschengeschlecht über diese Frage zu beruhigen, und immer im Reich der Erscheinung bleiben dürfen. Übrigens sind diese dunklen Stellen in der Natur des Menschen für den Dichter und den tragischen insbesondere nicht leer, und noch weniger für den Redner, und in der Darstellung der Leidenschaften machen sie kein kleines Moment aus.

Thus it appears that Schiller, as a tragedian, and a rhetor,

[1] Helene Raff, *Ältere und neuere Wallenstein-Literatur* in the *Deutsche Rundschau*, clxviii (1916), p. 306.

consents to make capital out of his own philosophical ignorance.

Goethe's attitude on the question of free will, which involves the question of guilt, was, in 1799 as at other times, pretty well defined. In his letter of July 31, which called forth Schiller's already quoted reply, he gives his views of *Paradise Lost* and adds

Unter andern Betrachtungen bei diesem Werke war ich auch genötigt, über den *freien Willen*, über den ich mir sonst nicht leicht den Kopf zerbreche, zu denken; er spielt in dem Gedicht, so wie in der christlichen Religion überhaupt, eine schlechte Rolle. Denn sobald man den Menschen von Haus aus für gut annimmt, so ist der freie Wille das alberne Vermögen aus Wahl vom Guten abzuweichen und sich dadurch *schuldig* zu machen: nimmt man aber den Menschen natürlich als bös an, oder, eigentlicher zu sprechen, in dem tierischen Falle unbedingt von seinen Neigungen hingezogen zu werden, so ist alsdann der freie Wille freilich eine vornehme Person, die sich anmasst, aus Natur gegen die Natur zu handeln.

These words give us the lead we require in considering briefly Goethe's treatment of the Faust legend. '*Faust*', says Carlyle in his *Life of Schiller*, 'is but a careless effusion compared with *Wallenstein*.' Perhaps even Carlyle would hardly dare to put the point in such a summary fashion to-day, yet we probably all know what he means. Every scene of *Wallenstein* is as carefully calculated as is every figure in a modern budget. *Faust* seems to have grown like an oak from an acorn and some of its boughs are gnarled and twisted by the winds of sixty winters. Yet every leaf of the tree springs from the same acorn and every line of *Faust* from the teeming brain of the master, young or old, whose name was Goethe. In the work of these sixty years we trace growth and change, and Goethe himself once exclaimed: 'Ei, bin ich denn achtzig Jahre alt geworden, um immer dasselbe denken zu müssen?' Yet, in the main, it is but the growing mastery of reason and will over emotion and passion, an evolution of the whole man, not a revolution within him. Storm and Stress he knew and put to profit both in his life and in his works, but the deepest depths of his mind, like those of Winkelmann's sea, remained 'allezeit ruhig', save perhaps for a short period in his boyhood, when he battled with the riddle of Evil. Quite early he won through to faith in the final victory of Good and in the essential goodness of man. As that great scholar, Konrad Burdach, has recently put it,[1] 'er war und blieb im Grunde doch immer ein Abkömmling der Humanitätslehre und des normativen Idealismus der Aufklärungszeit'. No man's character, least of all Goethe's, can be confined within the narrow bounds of a single sentence, but if we were forced to express our opinion of him in a score of words we might say, 'Goethe, being a good man, believes in man's essential goodness and in the triumph of Good over Evil through human effort.' Like Hamlet he held that

> There's a divinity that shapes our ends,
> Rough hew them how we will.

But as he presses forward on the path of experience, the idea of the 'Dämon' which urges Egmont along his dizzy path and drives Tasso to overstep the limits laid down by convention and propriety and Faust to turn in loathing from the dusty rutted roads of traditional learning begins to recede before the conception of a Higher Power in the hollow of whose hand, as in that of Buddha in the Chinese legend of Buddha and the monkey, lie the four corners of the vast earth. This is no blind Fate, raising and crushing man like a plaything; it is a Will that wills man's good, but trusts him to seek it for himself amid temptation, error, spiritual distress, and bitter repentance. Thus 'Schicksal' appears as the working together of the Creator and the created towards an end which both desire; but to the one the end is clear and certain, while the other is indeed conscious of his aim, but moves towards it gropingly 'in seinem dunklen Drange'.

[1] *Euphorion*, xxvii (1926), p. 65.

The question of 'Schuld', at first sight much more difficult, may perhaps be resolved by a bold argument. The idea is an instrument in the hands of God, a saving concept in the mind of man, a form of spiritual life, a mirror for the soul. But as a 'Ding-an-sich', to borrow, and perhaps to twist, the Kantian phrase, it has no meaning or existence. Guilt is a necessity of thought and feeling, and the word 'guilty' implies a system of ethics for which in human affairs there is everything to be said from a practical point of view. But from the point of view of one who does not, at bottom, regard man as capable of any but minor variations from the norm established by his own character it is a word of comparatively little significance in the great world-order. The saving premise to hold fast to here is that man as a creature is, essentially, of the same type as his Creator, only endowed with a lesser degree of intelligence. He is, in Leibniz' terminology, a monad of the higher type, a 'vernünftige Seele', 'a Geist' and an 'Ebenbild Gottes'.[1] As such he is active and acts, with more or less illumination, according to his nature. Goethe shares with Herakleitos the conviction ἦθος ἀνθρώπῳ δαίμων and with Leibniz the belief in a God who helps or hinders us as he sees fit, while we, like children, seek to create or destroy, as seems good to us.

This explains to us the comparative absence in *Faust* of the concept of guilt. Faust himself acts according to his nature, given the temptations which God himself permits Mephisto to throw in his path. Even in his treatment of Gretchen there is nothing inhuman, nothing unnatural, though the consequences are tragic, and for a time, at least, 'Reue' inevitably fills his breast. But, in the general plan of the poem, as a whole, this sense of guilt plays only a short-lived role. Faust passes on

durch Seligkeit und Schuld der Gretchen-Liebe zum idealen Hochzeitsbunde mit Helena, von der antiken Heroine dann zur

[1] Cf. K. Burdach's essay (cited above), pp. 12 f., and *Faust* i. 516.

Erkenntnis und Bewährung des Satzes: 'Die Tat ist alles,' und
zuletzt im Tatkampf gegen die zwecklose Wut der Elemente, im
Tatsieg über das Meer, dem durch Deiche Land für freie Arbeit
abgerungen wird, zur Niederlage Mephistos, zur Rettung
Faustens.

These words of Burdach's (*ibid.*, p. 19) form an admirable
conclusion to my brief argument.

One more point may be made before we pass on. Many
of us may have felt, some may even have regretted, the comparative absence in *Faust* of tragic tension. May it not be
best explained upon the lines indicated? Professor Richard
Wilhelm of Frankfurt-am-Main in *The Review of Nations*
(No. 1, Geneva, January, 1927) has recently attempted to
distinguish the characters created by Goethe from those of
Shakespeare as possessing something more lyrical, more living, more irrational, less ruled by inflexible necessity. This is
a theory which an Englishman finds it hard to share. But the
professor goes on to admit that there is a certain distant
resemblance between the works of Goethe and the poetry of
the Chinese. The resemblance shows itself in the acceptance
of certain types of character which react typically and normally to certain typical situations. 'Side by side with the type
of the upright man there exists the type of the bandit, the
traitor, the beggar.' There is a 'right way' for each of them
to act in a given situation and each of them acts in it according to his type. 'Chinese wisdom excludes the tragic' from its
purview, and this exclusion extends even to the tragic in
poetry; for here, too, 'all is reduced to type', and what we call
'dramatic movement' becomes of minor importance beside
the 'astonishing richness in the painting of characters and
situations'. Faust is a good man, and the good man's life,
being essentially attuned to the world-order, cannot end in
tragedy, although there may be in it what Goethe himself
described as 'irreducible fractions'. One good man may
have a hard lot, another an easy one, one may be 'von

F

Schicksal verwahrlost und beschädigt', like Karl Philipp
Moritz, another, like himself, 'begünstigt und vorgezogen'
by the same power, but they are none the less spiritual
brothers 'von derselben Art', both 'gut' and 'vernünftig', each
'nach seiner Art' striving ceaselessly toward the goal of a
higher humanity.[1] Goethe, we may admit, recognizes, as all
clear-sighted men do, both the vengeance exacted upon guilt
by itself and the misfortune that may fall to the lot even
of him who strives. But in his greatest dramatic poem he
refuses to be frightened by the gloomy spectres of sin and
damnation. Salvation is to him who fights against the Powers
of Darkness, for God is in his Heaven and man, his 'Ebenbild',
is after all more 'göttlich' than 'tierisch'. The early Prome-
thean Faust has the power to become truly a man, 'edel,
hilfreich und gut'. He makes friends with fate itself, and his
guilt towards the individual is blotted out by his service of
humanity. And so we feel in reading the poem as Goethe felt
in contemplating the majesty of the Alps, 'Das Erhabene gibt
der Seele die schöne Ruhe'. Beholding the finished work,
despite its gaps and sudden changes of level, we may add,
'Man fühlt tief, hier ist nichts Willkürliches, [sondern] alles
langsam bewegendes ewiges Gesetz. . .'[2]

In Hölderlin's *Empedokles* (1799), to which I would now
turn for a moment, we find the same rule of law and right,
only in plainer, more self-conscious terms. Moriz Enzinger
in his valuable and stimulating, if sometimes too summary,
lecture on *Das deutsche Schicksalsdrama* (Innsbruck, 1922) expressed a widely held view of Hölderlin in the words, 'Bei ihm
ist der Anschluss an die Antike am deutlichsten, bei ihm aber
auch der Schicksalsgedanke am krassesten.' The first half of
this sentence seems to me to be happier than the second, so
far as *Empedokles* is concerned, but we do certainly find in this
drama that fate and guilt are interwoven with a degree of force

---

[1] Cf. Burdach's citations from Goethe, *ibid.*, pp. 22 f.
[2] *Ibid.*, pp. 45 f. (Weimar ed. iv. 4, pp. 70–2).

and conviction that is perhaps unsurpassed in German poetry. The poet of that terribly moving *Schicksalslied* in *Hyperion* was not likely to exclude fate from his drama, but here, as indeed in *Hyperion* itself, when we regard it carefully, we find that human error, human wilfulness, human arrogance, is the root of the hero's misfortune. And it is his strong sense of guilt, coupled with his sense that the 'Göttersprüche' must be fulfilled

> Und, wie die Sterne, geht unaufgehalten
> Das Leben im Vollendungsgange weiter—

that leads him to his self-chosen act of self-destruction. He can say, at the last, to his disciple Pausanias

> Bin ich durch Sterbliche doch nicht bezwungen
> Und geh in meiner Kraft furchtlos hinab
> Den selbst erkornen Pfad; mein Glück ist dies.
> Mein Vorrecht ists.

But this proud boast is the boast of a prophet who has lived through 'den Tag der Unehr' and cannot claim that he himself has been wholly void of offence towards both 'Sterbliche und Götter', though, at the end, he is with both 'versöhnt'. His once had been

> Des Mannes Stimme, der sich mehr
> Denn Sterbliche gerühmt, weil ihn zu viel
> Beglückt die gütige Natur.

He had felt within him 'die stumme, todesöde Brust', and, having arrogantly called the gods themselves his servants, had been forced to cry out in his bitter repentance

> O glaub' es mir, ich wäre lieber nicht
> Geboren.

His plunge into Etna is for him, at the last, a way of salvation, a path 'zu neuer Jugend', but before he felt it thus it had already appeared to him as the path of necessity:

> Ich gehe meines Weges, Kritias,
> Und weiss wohin, und schämen muss ich mich,
> Dass ich gezögert bis zum äussersten.
> Was musst' ich auch so lange warten,
> Bis Glück und Geist und Jugend wich und nichts
> Wie Torheit überblieb und Elend.
> . . . . . Aber nun ists not!

Only in the end, and after deep spiritual suffering, this necessity is greeted by the seer as the deepest, purest joy. And Panthea cries with fullest right

> Nicht in der Blüt' und Purpurtraub'
> Ist heilige Kraft allein, es nährt
> Das Leben vom Leide sich, Schwester!
> Und trinkt, wie mein Held, doch auch
> Am Todeskelche sich glücklich!

Fate and guilt alike have here been swallowed up in Death, and Death itself in the glory of the life beyond the tomb in the gleaming Æther where dwell in purity the gods and demi-gods:

> So musst es geschehen.
> So will es der Geist
> Und die reifende Zeit,
> Denn Einmal bedurften
> Wir Blinden des Wunders.

'Wunder', not one but many, are among the clearest signs of the 'Schicksalsdrama' which became popular in the first third of the nineteenth century. They are not, of course, an invention of that age, but merely a revival of a fashion. Carlyle remarked with one-sided irony that 'about the time of *Wallenstein's* appearance we of this gifted land were shuddering at *The Castle Spectre*'. The odd thing is that long after 1799 the Germans were shuddering at their own castle spectres and family ghosts, and that the earlier history of this type of play may be traced back to the baroque age in modern

times and in some sort also to medieval legend, still more
perhaps to Seneca, and in part at least to the Greek drama.
Moreover, Schiller himself produced, after *Wallenstein*, one
play which, as Professor Willoughby has remarked in his
brief account of *The Classical Age of German Literature*, must
in a sense be regarded as 'an undoubted forerunner of
the "Schicksalstragödie" '.[1] The strong influence of *Oedipus
Tyrannus* on *Die Braut von Messina*, however, appears to me to
be quite undeniable, while the methods of the author here
remind me of Voltaire no less than of Corneille, for every
entrance and exit, every silence and every revelation, is calculated with the most extreme mathematical precision. The
result is that the responsibility for the murder of Don Manuel
is the joint outcome of the interaction of love, hatred, and fate,
but it is not quite clear to me that we are justified in calling
this fate either 'accident' or 'blind fate'. Schiller might have
claimed that what Donna Isabella herself describes as 'Glück'
when she says in Act IV

> Vieles gelang mir! Viel auch tat das Glück!

is nothing more nor less than that Ananke in which the Greeks
believed. And he might have cited Herder's remarks on the
doctrines of Empedocles from the Essay on *Liebe und Selbstheit*:

> Durch Hass, sagte er (Empedocles) werden die Dinge getrennt
> und jedes *Einzelne* bleibt was es ist; durch Liebe werden sie ver-
> bunden und gesellen sich zueinander, sofern sie sich nämlich,
> ihrer Natur nach, gesellen können; denn freilich, auch über die
> Liebe, sagten die Griechen, herrscht das *Schicksal*; und *Notwendig-
> keit*, die älteste der Gottheiten, ist mächtiger, als die Liebe.

My point is that for him who believes truly in the goddess
Ananke these so-called chances and accidents are neither
more nor less than unexpected and unusual ways in which the
will of this goddess, 'the eldest of the divine beings', is wrought
out. Schiller again appears to me to be making use, as a

---

[1] Oxford University Press, 1926, p. 124.

dramatist, of an age-old conception of necessity, which he is
not concerned here to reconcile philosophically with his
belief in the freedom of the human will. The only valid
objection to the play seems to be that it strains our credulity
to believe that the truth would not have been, in actual life,
revealed in time to prevent the tragedy. To this Schiller
might perhaps reply that the tragedy consists partly in the
fact that Donna Isabella and her children are of the type
of family, not wholly rare, perhaps, in which explanations
never are made at the right time! In any case Schiller has
chosen, as before, to divide the responsibility for the tragic
ending between passionate human hearts and a passionless
higher power, but we rather beg the question when we call
this higher power 'blind'.

May I add that I am far from convinced that Schiller
wholly invented the outlines of his fable? I believe rather
that he must have at some time known, and later forgotten
that he had known, the legend of the hostile brothers of
Bornhofen, and that he fused this tale with some Greek story
of incestuous love between brother and sister, transferring
the scene to Sicily, but retaining the medieval period and,
of course, adding nearly all the poetry. This legend is known
to me, at present, only in the version printed by Kieser,
where it bears the title *Die feindlichen Brüder*, and supplies the
subject of a striking engraving facing the title of the work.[1]
Dr. Buchheim pointed out that Heine probably knew the
tale from oral tradition, and Schiller might have done the
same. The point is one that deserves further investigation,
especially in view of Karoline von Wolzogen's statement that
Schiller expressed the view that 'am Rhein . . . sei der passendste Platz für ein solches Gemälde des Menschengeschicks
in seiner Allgemeinheit'. This legend, at least, turns upon
the jealousy of the two brothers, who have long quarrelled
over their shares of their father's property and have the ill

[1] Kieser, *Die Sagen des Rheinlandes von Basel bis Rotterdam*, 3. Aufl., Mainz, 1870.

luck to fall in love with the same lady and forthwith fight
a duel. The last sentence implies that they are under a curse:

Sowie auf allen Taten des unnatürlichen Bruderpaares, so
ruhete der Unstern auch auf diesem Kampfe. In blinder Wut
rannten sie, zugleich aufeinander losstürzend, einer in des andern
Schwert, und endeten beide zur selben Stunde ihr verruchtes
Dasein.

Yet even *Die Braut von Messina*, be its origin what it may,
shows the clearest characteristic of the classical German
tragedy—the tragedy of Goethe, of Schiller, even of Hölderlin—its serenity, a serenity which comes of the conviction that
the 'moral law within', like 'the starry heavens above',
depends upon a world-order and a world-will, which the man
of intelligence and of good-will can but deem right and just.
The writers of the Fate-drama, on the other hand, seem to
be obsessed with the feeling, not unknown to certain of the
Hebrew prophets, that, in our world at least, it is rather
the rule than the exception that the sins of the fathers should
be visited upon the children, even to the third and fourth
generation. They seem to reverse the saying of the Koran
and hold that *more* will be exacted of a man than he himself
has deserved. They are super-occidental in their outlook,
whereas Goethe, Schiller, and even Hölderlin have more
affinity with the higher type of oriental thought. This judgement may seem far from obvious, but I am led to it by some
words of Professor Paul Masson-Oursel (in *The Review of
Nations*, No. 1). 'L'oriental croit,' he says, 'pour parler
comme Leibniz, que "c'est partout comme ici", autrement
dit que les conditions de l'autre vie ne diffèrent que peu des
conditions de la vie présente; d'où sa sérénité que nous pre-
nons trop souvent pour fatalisme.' We recall that Goethe,
Schiller, and Hölderlin are all, more or less, under the influence of Leibniz. The writers of the 'Schicksalsdrama'
are rather indebted to the sources Professor Masson-Oursel
enumerates when he adds, 'Il a fallu les indignations des

Prophètes, les terreurs apocalyptiques, l'âme bouillonnante d'Israël pour semer en nos âmes de Méditerranéens un insolite "romantisme" de l'au-delà.' They have, too, the taste for the occult, from which the true Orientals, according to this authority, are, contrary to the common notion, really exempt.

Enzinger has recently drawn attention to the strong traditional element in the 'Schicksalsdrama' proper. I need not dwell upon its affinities with the 'Ritterdrama' and the drama of the baroque period, notably of Gryphius, whose tragedies, by the way, have long been underrated. Perhaps, from the psychological point of view, we may say that in the ' Schicksalsdrama' crime tends to become more important than character and symbols begin to outweigh reasons. The unconscious urge displaces the conscious plan. The authors themselves seem to be obsessed with the dramatic, even the theatrical, strikingness of crimes and punishments. They cry out, Why this punishment? Why this crime? How could the hero do the horrible deed? And the easy, obvious answer is 'the curse, the fate, the divine wrath'. Their theology reverts to the Hebrew type; they combine with it also, perhaps, the Christian conception of the innocent being punished for the sins of the guilty. They believe, before Darwin, and unscientifically, in the power of heredity. They widen the medieval concept of the criminal as one possessed of the devil,[1] so as to let the descendant release the ancestor by paying the penalty. They have a notable belief in the solidarity of the family, drawn partly from Greek, partly from Hebrew mythology and sociology, partly also perhaps, as Enzinger suggests, from the clannishness of the colonists in the eastern part of Germany.

Leaving aside Grillparzer's early play, *Die Ahnfrau*, there is perhaps only one drama of this type that is worth dwelling

---

[1] See the article by Hans Fehr, *Mehr Geistesgeschichte in der Rechtsgeschichte*, *Deutsche Vierteljahrsschrift*, Jan. 1927 (5. Jahrg., pp. 1–8).

upon here, *Der vierundzwanzigste Februar* (1810). Its author, Zacharias Werner, was born in Königsberg in 1768, two years earlier than Hölderlin, and grew up under influences, such as those of freemasonry and mysticism, which are much older than Romanticism, but easily unite with that spirit. He belonged to what Freiherr von Knigge in his *Umgang mit den Menschen* had called 'die Enthusiasten, überspannten, romanhaften Menschen, Kraft-Genies und excentrischen Leute'. He would probably have been included by Knigge among the 'Andächtler, Frömmler, Heuchler', certainly among the 'abergläubische Leute, die an Ammen-Märchen, Gespenster-Histörchen und dergleichen hängen', and perhaps even among the poets who offer the audience 'im Schauspielhause keine Nahrung für den Geist, sondern nur Zeitverkürzung und sinnlichen Genuss'; but here he would have judged too harshly and narrowly, for Werner is a true poet in his own genre, whether one cares for the genre or no, and his talent won the admiration of Schiller and even Goethe, as well as of Grillparzer. Bielschowsky's remark that Goethe 'hat sich davon einen Augenblick blenden lassen' hardly gives the truth in full. There is a force about this one-act play which Goethe probably knew better than Bielschowsky how to appreciate. The mere fact that it has frequently been dismissed as a 'Schicksalstragödie' should blind no one to its merits since Jacob Minor's discussion of this type of drama put criticism on a sounder basis.[1]

The subject, be it admitted, is painful, but it is handled, as Minor rightly remarked, 'mit meisterhafter Kunst'. 'Stimmung' and character are equally well created. 'Den Druck und das Schuldbewusstsein, welches auf seiner eigenen Seele lastete, weiss er seinen unter der Wucht des Schicksals erliegenden Personen einzuflössen'. And, as Minor does not

[1] See also M. Koch, *Gesch. d. deutschen Lit.* (Leipzig, 1911), p. 217 on Werner's 'stimmungs- und kraftvoll durchgeführten Einfall', which was caricatured and turned into 'ein albernes System' by Houwald and Müllner in their much less inspired works. For Minor see below, p. 78.

fail to point out, the poet walks firmly along the precipitous narrow path of high tragedy where a false step would have tumbled him into the abyss of the ridiculous.

This metaphor rises to our minds of itself when we think of the place which Werner chose for the action of his play, high up in a lonely Alpine inn on the Gemmi pass, that rears its wall of rock thousands of feet above the Baths of Leuk. 'Das einer Mörderhöhle ähnliche Schwarrbach' is Werner's description of the place, which, of course, he had visited. Perhaps only those who have stood on this pass at nightfall and seen the sun go down on the gleaming glaciers and the wild dark rocky peaks can wholly enter into the 'Stimmung' of the play, in which only three persons take part, unless we count Nature herself as the fourth and greatest. The plot, in itself, is perfectly simple—if you will, *banal*. Aristotle would perhaps call it a drama in which a father unwittingly murders his own son, despite the entreaties of the mother, for the sake of his gold, and the recognition takes place at the moment in which the deed is accomplished. Whether Aristotle would have approved of the play I do not know: but I think a sound modern critic would discern in it the same kind of power that one gets in Strindberg. The case is exaggerated, almost unique, but profoundly undeniable, irresistible, like life itself, in such a place. The curse on Kunz Kuruth, the knife he had thrown at his own father, the brand of Cain on his baby-boy, the boy's accidental cutting of his sister's throat, each misfortune on the 24th of February, Kuruth's curse on *his* son, the return of the wanderer, on the same day of the year, twenty years later, only to be killed by his father with the same big knife, as the clock strikes twelve—it might so easily have all seemed ridiculous, just as to some audiences Strindberg's *Ghost Sonata* seems frantic nonsense. But the whole is saved by the poetry of language and the high seriousness of the author's tone. 'Vieles im Recht,' says Hans Fehr, 'ist unbewusst, triebmässig geschaffen worden, daher auch der Logik häufig

nicht zugänglich. Es ist prälogisch, wie Levy-Brühl so gut
sagt. Aber stets sind es geistige Kräfte, welche zunächst die
Dinge in der Rechtswelt hervorrufen.' It is the same in the
popular conception of crime and punishment, guilt and fate.
And now and then arises a poet like Werner who puts a
popular conception into true poetic form and language.

We see that we must have done with that narrow-minded
attitude to literature which inquires first, last, and always,
How could these things be? and failing to find a reasonable
explanation merely condemns. It is as narrow-minded as
that of the art critic who cannot decide whether a picture is
beautiful till he has determined whether the legs are in
normal proportion to the trunk. The anomalous has its place
in literature as well as in life. The incredible story or play
may be incredibly beautiful: perhaps, in a sense, incredibly
true.

I have spoken of Werner's use of a popular conception.
It is also one form of religious attitude: *prorsus credible, quia
ineptum est* is a phrase which represents a certain type of mind
found perhaps as frequently in literature as in the Church.
Where science ends mysticism begins. It is an old religious
doctrine that God is inscrutable and his ways past finding
out. And Werner's soul was religious, as well as sensual.
Such minds can often reconcile the ideas of curse and guilt,
God and fate, where the rationalist flounders in antinomies.
Werner makes Kunz Kuruth read in the Bible, the moment
before the big knife falls

'Des Vaters Segen bauet den Kindern Häuser,
Aber der Mutter Fluch reisst sie wieder nieder.'—
Nicht wahr!—Der Mutter Segen baut allein
Sie auf; des Vaters Fluch, der reisst sie ein!

Kunz, be it noted, believes that the stranger has committed
a murder himself and is therefore 'vogelfrei':

Ihn töten könnt' ich—darnach kräht kein Hahn!
Beim Mörder steht das jedem frei.

He looks upon himself as the executor of law and justice, even as the defender of the Eidgenossenschaft, if he kills the stranger, yet he has qualms and would wish to die 'schuldlos'. He is warned by a vision, the ghost of his father sitting in the arm-chair, turning round to gaze at him, 'blau, mit gebrochenen Augen'. He even prays, confusedly, 'Vater unser, der mich hat verflucht!' But he will not leave his (earthly) salvation to God, even if he must for ever repent it. The deed is done, the recognition complete the moment after, and the dying son exclaims:

> Vergeben
> Hat euch der Vater! Ihr seid fluchentsühnt!

Kunz asks and receives his son's forgiveness, but his soul is not yet happy, for God is in his heaven, and the last lines mingle the thoughts of crime, justice, and the grace of God:

*Kunz.* Und Gott vergibt er?!
*Kurt.* Amen—!
*Trude.* Er stirbt!
*Kunz.*                    Wohlan—in Gottes Namen!
Ich büsse gern das, was ich schwer verdient!
Ich geh' zum Blutgericht und geb' die Mordtat an!
Wenn ich durch's Henkerbeil bin abgetan,
Dann mag Gott richten—ihm ist alles offenbar!
Das war ein vierundzwanzigster Februar!
Ein Tag ist's!—Gottes Gnad' ist ewig! Amen!

Here too, then, the religious concept prevails, Fate, like guilt, is but an aspect of the will of God. The theological difficulty is not resolved, the popular 'Anschauungen' are not explained, but dramatically exploited.

As for the signs and wonders, the knife, the fatal date, the curses, have we not here simply a reversion to the common concepts of primitive religion? The struggle is, as in *Faust* and in the medieval ordeals, between God and the Devil. The concept of an evil fate is a way of conceiving the powers of darkness that fight against the powers of light. The idea

of God is Christian-Hebrew, that of Fate is probably older
still, the two are interwoven, as still in some forms of popular
belief. There is a slice of the savage in most of us yet. Dr.
Marett has remarked that 'the savage is not perpetually
spook-haunted', and the less savage we are, the less spook-
haunted we generally are. But there are crises in life in which
'one is at one's wits' end . . . the ordinary and expected has
been replaced by the extraordinary and unexpected . . . we
are projected into the world of the unknown.' It is here that
religion may help, but also here that superstition and magic
find in some minds a strong response. Zacharias Werner
seems to me to have made not only a masterly, but even
a fully justifiable use of the survival of primitive mentality
and primitive symbols in his play. His means are different
from, but parallel to, the Prologue in Heaven and the concept of Mephisto in Goethe's *Faust*.

This brings me to my final point. Is it possible for a
Theistic, still more for a Christian, dramatist to produce
a fully tragic tragedy? The possibility has been categorically
denied by Leopold Ziegler in his study *Zur Metaphysik des
Tragischen* (Leipzig, 1902). He concludes his argument by
urging that the belief in personal immortality and future bliss
takes the sting out of death itself. Moreover, the concept of
an almighty God, who is necessarily wise and good, seems to
render human tragedy unreal. (We may feel that the only
true Christian tragedy would be to be cut off for ever from
the Divine favour.) 'In the last analysis it is Theism,' Ziegler
says, 'which destroys the tragic character of the process of
existence.' And he claims that 'die angewandte christliche
Mythe in Fausts Himmelfahrt erstickt die Tragik'. If this
view be correct, and I incline strongly to accept it, we may
say that, illogically, but with a true sense for the dramatic,
the writers of the 'Schicksalsdrama', notably Werner, have
found in the concept of the fateful and the fated a means of
introducing into their Christian dramas an essential element

of tension which would otherwise have been lacking. Hölderlin's *Empedokles*, on the other hand, is a good example of the
theistic drama in which 'die Wucht des transzendentalen
Optimismus jede emporkeimende Regung des Schmerzes
unterdrückt' and in which 'der Tod nur noch Lustgefühl
auslöst' in the soul of the hero, so that the sense of the tragic
is swallowed up in the sense of religious ecstasy as we approach the last scenes of the play.[1]

[1] The quotations from Hölderlin's *Empedokles* are all taken from the 'erste
Fassung' (Zinkernagel's edition of the *Werke*, vol. iii, pp. 19–109), the spelling
being slightly modernized.—The passage from Dr. R. R. Marett's *Anthropology*,
cited at p. 77 above, will be found on p. 211 of the 1921 reprint.—*Das
Schicksalsdrama* ed. by Jakob Minor (vol. 151 of Kürschner's *Deutsche National-
literatur*) contains Werner's play. Minor's introduction is supplemented by
his article in the *Jahrbuch der Grillparzer-Gesellschaft*, vol. ix (1899). Cf. R.
Arnold, *Das deutsche Drama* (München, 1925), pp. 531 and 551.

# IV

# HERDER'S INFLUENCE ON THE METRICAL VERSION OF HÖLDERLIN'S *HYPERION*

*I. Die Weisen.*

THE brief, experimental metrical fragments of *Hyperion* have been the subject of much controversy, especially since Zinkernagel in *Die Entwicklung von Hölderlins Hyperion* (1907) subjected them to searching, but not wholly satisfactory, analysis. Perhaps the only clear facts about them are that they do express in iambic verse certain ideas that are also found in the prose versions, and that these ideas are mainly philosophical and based upon Plato's myth of the birth of Eros. On the order of the fragments, on the degree of originality, the sources other than Plato, and on the date of composition the authorities do not seem to be exactly agreed. Still less does agreement seem to have been reached in relating the metrical fragments to the various prose versions. If Zinkernagel went too far in splitting up the fragments into fresh versions, Cassirer (*Idee und Gestalt*, p. 113) helps us only a little by remarking—'Wenn bei irgendeinem Lyriker, so spürt man bei Hölderlin durch alle Verschiedenheit der dichterischen Stoffe und Vorwürfe hindurch den Rhythmus und den Pulsschlag ein und desselben lebendigen lyrischen Grundgefühls.' This reminder is valuable, but it need not deter us from studying the growth of *Hyperion* from its early stages to its complete form. For allowing the 'Grundton' to be the same here as there, and even in *Empedokles* and the philosophic essays, we may find it of interest and value to study this 'Grundton' and 'geistige Eigenart Hölderlins' (which no one pretends to minimize) in its reactions to outward stimulus of different sorts. To change the metaphor to an art that seems closer to literature, the main theme of a great picture may sometimes be followed through a dozen sketches

in which not only details, but even important figures or objects
shift their poses or positions as the artist struggles to work out
the idea in his mind and place it on the canvas in the most
satisfactory manner. In the end the chief idea very likely
remains unaltered, but the exact form, the values and the
colours, may all have changed. They will probably be richer,
they may be better, but that is not certain. As Hemsterhuis
writes in his *Lettre sur la Sculpture* (Œuvres, 2^me éd., 1809, i,
p. 21), 'La première idée distincte et bien conçue d'un
homme de génie, qui est rempli du sujet qu'il veut traiter, est
non-seulement bonne, mais déjà bien au-dessus de l'expression.' The elaboration of the sketch may damage its aesthetic
value, but each elaboration indicates some new idea of the
artist, some new sight of his theme, some fresh grappling with
the problem, never entirely to be solved, of translating the
picture seen only 'in the mind's eye' into the form in which
it becomes visible to others. The literary artist, above all,
is sensible to the stimulus of other writers, his thought is a
movement in a symphony, or rather, it is the music of one
player in an orchestra, each member of which is contributing
his share to a symphony which is taking shape all the time
and is never finished. Each player is limited by the capacities
of his own instrument and by his own musical abilities, which
include the ear not only for his own music, but for that of the
other musicians.

So much it seemed necessary to say in defence of the comparative and historical method of inquiry and its use in this
case. Cassirer himself employs it (*loc. cit.*, pp. 114 f.) when
he writes, 'Der gemeinsame Boden, von dem aus die Grund-
ansicht des speculativen Idealismus und die dichterische
und philosophische Weltauffassung Hölderlins erwächst, lässt
sich in den drei Namen Kant, Spinoza und Platon bezeich-
nen'. But, as he also points out, these three names are inadequate to explain Hölderlin any more than they do Fichte,
Schelling, and Hegel. There is always a tendency, and it is

very frequent in German writers, to overlook the importance of the less brilliant stars. To confine oneself here to Hölderlin, it seems fairly clear that the 'Grundton', to which Cassirer rightly draws attention, or, as I should prefer to call it, the 'Haupteinstellung des Geistes', the mental orientation normal to our poet, may have an explanation drawn from his mental life as well as from the original character of his mind at birth. Here, indeed, one touches upon a mystery and does well to speak with caution. Could one recapture the poet's earliest experiences one might, with the psycho-analysts, explain the poet's early pantheistic tendency by some sublimated sexual longing for union with some desired being.[1] But even confining ourselves to the known conscious life of the poet we can find in the Bible, in pietist hymns and works of edification, in the Latin authors, especially Lucretius and Cicero (*De Natura Deorum*) many 'Anhaltspunkte' on which a young poet, with a love of nature, could build for himself a poetic pantheism, even before falling in with the pre-Socratics and Plato and Spinoza and Jacobi. I have already drawn attention to the very strong influence of the Stoic philosophy, transmitted and emphasized very particularly by C. P. Conz. It remains, in connexion with the metrical fragments, to try to show that these were written under the influence not only of Schiller and possibly Fichte[2] and, of course, Plato, but also more clearly perhaps than in any but the last case, under that of Schiller's too much neglected predecessor, Herder. Herder leads us back to his own teachers, Hemsterhuis and Hamann, but also directly to Empedokles. It is possible, though it

---

[1] Jung in his *Psychology of the Unconscious* has dealt at some length with the longing 'to return to the mother', which he finds clearly indicated in many places in Hölderlin's poetry. See further my paper on *Hölderlin's Ideals in Hyperion and Empedokles*. My friend Professor W. Horn, in a note on H. Löns, states the main principle very succinctly in one sentence, 'Im dichterischen Schaffen wirken Bewusstes und Unbewusstes zusammen' (*Archiv. f. d. St. d. N. Sp. und. Lit.*, Bd. 145, p. 250).
[2] Cf. Zinkernagel, *Entwicklung &c.*, III. Kapitel, and more recently in *Literaturblatt für German. u. roman. Philol.*, 1929, cols. 254 f.

might be hard to prove, that Hölderlin's drama has its roots in the essay of Herder from which I shall quote.[1]

Whatever may be the correct order of the metrical fragments, their essence apparently lies in the narrative of the visit to 'the wise man' and in the fact that his philosophic view of the importance of nature, *as opposed and yet essential to reason*, made a very strong impression upon the narrator (the *ich* of these fragments). As Cassirer and most of his predecessors fully realize, it is the Platonic myth of the birth of Eros, as related by Diotima in the *Symposion*, round which the argument of the metrical version turns. The myth is used by Hölderlin to combat that form of idealism which denies the value of the feelings and into which his Hyperion had fallen. Zinkernagel (*Entwicklung*, p. 79) quite clearly holds that the first fragment (*S.W.*, ii. 245 f.) gives a picture, almost, as he says, a caricature, of the unfriendly features 'eines Kantischen Rigoristen', and Cassirer seems to follow him. This view seems to me barely tenable in the light of the importance attached by Kant to the role played by the senses in our mental and moral life. It may seem rash to differ from both these able critics in such a matter, but there is much to be considered here that makes against their view.

In the first place it is rather a superficial conception of Kant's ethics that accuses him of such exaggerated rigorism. For Kant does not teach us to destroy our feelings, and Schiller's famous epigram has somewhat the air of a cheap score. 'Kant lehrt ja nicht', August Messer remarks[2], 'dass man, um sittlich zu handeln, notwendig gegen die Neigung handeln müsse, oder dass gar alle Neigungen in uns ertötet

---

[1] It may seem strange that the part played by Herder in influencing Hölderlin should not have been more fully recognized. But such things are always occurring. However, Betzendörfer (1921) and Hoffmann (1918) have both recently called attention to 'die fundamentale Bedeutung Herders für Hölderlins Entwicklung'. Von Grolman also recognizes the importance of this connexion with Herder.

[2] *Gesch. d. Philos.*, ii. 141. (This work, though brief, is well weighed and authoritative.)

werden müssten . . . Gehen unsere Neigungen von selbst auf das objektiv Gute, so wird uns die Verwirklichung des Gewissensgebotes umso leichter fallen.' For this reason (and the point might easily be argued more fully), it is very difficult to apply Hölderlin's first fragment mainly or solely to Kant. In the second place, the narrator attributes his condition in the opening lines partly to Fate and partly to '*den Weisen*'.[1] I am unwilling to stress unduly the point that the speaker appears to be Hyperion and therefore a young Greek whose youth was past before Kant had published any of his critical works. But it must be pointed out that there is not a line on this page which does not apply better to a pupil of the Stoic and neo-Platonist and, to come to the moderns, of the Leibniz-Wolffian schools, than to a pupil of Kant.

Let us begin with the Stoics, whose very strong influence on Hölderlin I have already stressed in my *Hölderlin and the German Neohellenism* (Part I, ch. v). I need hardly dwell again on the importance, in the Stoic doctrines, of the idea of Fate ('Schiksal'), but the occurrence of the word in the first line of this fragment is certainly not accidental. I am more concerned to point out that, while honouring Nature in the abstract, the Stoics are specially famous for inculcating in the individual human being the neglect and contempt of natural feelings. This fact is so well known that I content myself with citing two or three sentences from Messer's account of this school.[2] Having pointed out that the severe ethics of the Stoics 'der asketischen Moral des Christentums vorarbeitete', Messer sums up their attitude to the passions in these terms, 'Als gefährlichste Feinde der Tugend galten die unvernünftigen Seelenregungen, die Affekte und Leiden-

---

[1] Gestählt vom Schiksaal *und den Weisen*, war
Durch meine Schuld mein jugendlicher Sin
Tyrannisch gegen die Natur geworden . . .
(*S.W.*, ed. Zinkernagel, ii, p. 245.)

[2] *Op. cit.*, i, 83. In Hölderlin's case Christian doctrine of course supported the Stoic outlook by preaching the mortification of the flesh. Cf. Lessing on Cronegk's *Olint und Sophronia* in the *Hamburg. Dramaturgie.*

schaften wie Lust, Begierde, Schmerz, Furcht. So ist die "Apathie", d. h. die Freiheit von der Herrschaft der Leidenschaften Voraussetzung der Tugend.' It is important to note further that Hölderlin's term 'die Weisen' is *the Stoic technical term* (in German form) for 'the Good' (since virtue depends on knowledge of right and wrong). These are elementary facts, known to all, but usually forgotten in dealing with the metrical fragment of *Hyperion*.

The so-called Eclectics of the Hellenistic-Roman period are as severe upon the senses as the Stoics themselves. Cicero in his *De Officiis* reproduces the views of Panaetius, and we find there (Bk. I. xx. 66–7) such statements as that 'fortitude has two characteristics. The first is indifference to outward circumstances . . . To regard honour as the only good and *to be free from passion* are the two fruits of this virtue.' It should not be forgotten that German ethics, even in Kant's day, were largely based on this work. Garve's version, made at the command of Frederick the Great, appeared in 1783, was in its fourth edition in 1792, and reached a sixth in 1819.[1]

Philo of Alexandria, combining Jewish with Greek learning, taught that God himself was unqualified Being, had no need of the world, and even after the Creation remained 'without suffering and without fear, having no part in evil, not to be influenced, without care, unwearied, full of unclouded blessedness'.[2] This comes very close to Hölderlin's picture of the 'selige Genien' in his *Schicksalslied*, the origin of which may go back to his early studies in philosophy and

---

[1] On Cicero in Germany at this time see G. B. Gardner's introduction to his translation of the *De Officiis*, p. xv. There were numerous school editions of this work, as of the *De Nat. Deorum*. See, for him and the Stoics, the bibliographies of Kayser, Engelmann, Tennemann, and Herzog-Hauck's *Enzyklop.* Note especially in this connexion the works of K. P. Conz, in particular his *Abhandlungen f. d. Gesch. u. d. Eigenthümliche der Späteren Stoischen Philos., nebst einem Versuche über Christliche, Kantische und Stoische Moral* (Tübingen, 1794). The *Philolog. Bibliothek* (Göttingen, 1770) promoted interest in Philo, &c.

[2] Cited by Messer (in German), *op. cit.*, ii. 91. Cf. *ibid.*, 92–5 for the neo-Platonists, pp. 99 f. for St. Augustine.

theology.[1] In his ethics, as Messer points out, Philo follows the sterner Stoics closely and demands that we should not only master, but should root out, our passions. It is important to note that Philo claimed to find this doctrine in the Old Testament, declaring that 'Moses teaches that one must cut out all passion from the soul and not merely moderate the passions, but become free from them'.

A somewhat similar asceticism is common to the neo-Platonists and also to St. Augustine.[2] The stages of soul-culture depend on overcoming the 'Hang zum Sinnlichen' (Messer), and it is worth noting that in the different orders of beings, heavenly, human, animal, and plant, we get precisely the contrasts mentioned by Hölderlin in this fragment, with the additional lowest stage to which he also refers in the final version of *Hyperion*. The moral life consists for Plotinus in freeing one's self from the senses and attaining to true knowledge. 'The disgrace of gold is in its being permeated with earthy matter . . . And so the soul; let it but be cleared of the desires that come by its too intimate commerce with the body, *emancipate from all the passions*,[3] purged from all that has accrued by its embodiment, withdrawn, a solitary, to itself again—in that moment the ugliness, that came only from the alien nature, is stripped away.'[4]

Of all the Church Fathers St. Augustine appears to have exerted the greatest influence, not less on the Protestants than on the Roman Catholics. And the ethics of St. Augustine are essentially ascetic. 'Er neigt dazu', Messer remarks,

---

[1] R. Kerber, *Hölderlins Verhältnis zu Homer* (Leipzig, 1924), p. 32, suggests Homer's gods as model, but admits a difference. 'Seelige Genien' are scarcely θεοί, but rather demigods.

[2] Students of philosophy and theology are so fully aware of these facts that I may well be accused of writing *crambe repetita*. My only excuse is that it seems essential, once for all, to make it clear that Hölderlin's 'Die Weisen' cannot be reduced to Kant!

[3] Cf. Hölderlin's phrase, 'Der leidensfreie, reine Geist . . .' (*S.W.Z.* ii). The italics in the text are mine.

[4] Plot. *Enn.* i, 6. 5, tr. by S. McKenna.

'in der Sinnlichkeit, insbesondere in dem Geschlechtstrieb, etwas Sündhaftes zu sehen.'[1]

We need not follow this doctrine through the Middle Ages, though it colours much of the thought of the mystics. It is more important to glance here at the intellectualism which in metaphysics forms the normal counterpart to asceticism in ethics. The primacy of the reason, very strongly held in ancient and medieval times, notably by the neo-Platonists and by Thomas Aquinas, was not broken down by the Renaissance, and even Melanchthon's espousal of the Aristotelian philosophy and its consequent popularity in the Protestant universities led only towards a new (less idealistic) form of Rationalism. Man's soul is distinguished from that of the animals, according to Aristotle, precisely by the possession of reason ($\nu o \hat{v} s$). His happiness consists, moreover, in the 'rational' activity of his soul; and this was easily interpreted, like the doctrine of the mean, in a narrow, puritanical, or pietist manner. On the other hand, the mystics, even the enlightened Nicolas of Kues, though they set the *intuitio dei* above reason itself, had as low or a still lower opinion of the senses than the Rationalists. Nor had the views of Nicolas, Giordano Bruno, or even Jacob Böhme much influence on the official philosophy of the German universities before the discussion of Spinoza became a burning question about 1790.

Of Spinoza it must suffice to say here[2] that he was generally looked upon as an atheist and that, in any case, his theory of ethics is at once determinist and rooted in the *amor intellectualis dei*. And the adept in this would be precisely the

---

[1] Messer points out in his footnote that the unfortunate effect of this teaching is still at work in the Christian church. 'Sie (diese Lehre) hat verschuldet, dass als *unrein und tierisch* gilt, was als Quell alles Menschenlebens uns ehrwürdig und heilig sein sollte; ebenso, dass man in der Erziehung das Sexuelle meist totschweigt.' I well remember from my own childhood a sermon by a young preacher who represented the body as a sort of evil prison-house of the soul. F. Zinkernagel has recently called attention to the possibility of Hölderlin having been attracted by Gnosticism. (*Literaturblatt f. germ. und roman. Philol.* 1929, col. 254).     [2] On another side to Spinoza see p. 91 below.

'leidensfreie reine Geist', whom Hölderlin proceeds to criticize from the new point of view represented by the 'wise man'. The real 'schoolmen' of the modern period were Descartes, Leibniz, and Wolff. Descartes is the representative *par excellence* of modern rationalism, Descartes far more than Kant, whose first great *Kritik* was no less directed against pure rationalism than against pure sensualism. With Leibniz the most important philosophical problem of the eighteenth century begins to be fought out; and with Kant the campaign is ended by a compromise, in which the rational and the irrational are admitted to be equally necessary, and feeling is restored to a place of honour which it had scarcely enjoyed since the days of Plato.[1] It is Kant, in fact, rather than Leibniz, who revives the position of Plato, as Wilhelm Wundt has clearly declared:

Aus reinen Begriffen lässt sich keine Wirklichkeit aufbauen—das ist das Grundthema, das in Kants Kritik der überlieferten dialektischen Metaphysik bei allen den einzelnen metaphysischen Ideen wiederkehrt.

It is Kant who first clearly delimits the boundaries of knowledge:

man merkt (bei Kant) . . . das vornehmlich unter dem Einfluss der Naturwissenschaften und der empirischen Richtungen der Philosophie mächtiger gewordene Streben, die Erfahrung als letzte Erkenntnisquelle in ihre Rechte einzusetzen . . . (Es) lässt sich gerade von Kant sagen, dass er durch sein Streben, zwischen Empirismus und Rationalismus gewissermassen den "ehrlichen

---

[1] I am glad to find myself here in substantial agreement with the views of Alfred Bäumler, whose work, *Kants Kritik der Urteilskraft, ihre Geschichte und Systematik*, Bd. i, Halle, 1923, only came into my hands when I had reached this point in my essay. It appears to me to be of the first importance for the understanding of Kant's position and his approach to it, and it supplements, from the philosophical side, J. G. Robertson's *Studies in the Genesis of the Romantic Theory in the Eighteenth Century*. The existence of these two books relieves me of the task of tracing, in detail, the tradition of which the stages, in Germany, are expressed by Bäumler as 'Leibniz—die (deutsche) Ästhetik—Kant'. Hölderlin's position, one may say, is that of 'opposite number' to Hegel (for whom see Bäumler's *Einleitung*, p. 16). They both proceed from Kant tangentially, at different angles from Fichte's and Schelling's, and closer to one another.

Makler" zu spielen, nicht ganz unbeträchtliche Nachwirkungen der ältesten Gestaltung dialektischer Metaphysik, der Platonischen, erkennen lässt, wie man ja auch umgekehrt in dem wunderbaren Dialog, in dem Plato vorzugsweise der Erkenntnistheorie nahe tritt, in dem *Theätet*, schon die Anfänge einer kunstvoll geübten kritischen Methode finden kann.[1]

A tendency towards a higher estimate of the aesthetic faculty or judgement is to be found already in Leibniz. Hence one may be a little doubtful whether he is to be numbered among 'die Weisen' who had taught the young Hyperion to distrust the senses. 'Spinozas Philosophie', as Bäumler says,[2] 'hatte für das *Problem* des Irrationalen keinen Platz', whereas Leibniz recognized clearly the existence of this problem. But the 'modernity' of Leibniz in this matter was not obvious even in Kant's day, and Kant attacked him unhesitatingly for his excessive intellectualism in the *Kritik der reinen Vernunft*. Many passages might be cited, but the following will suffice.

*Leibniz intellektuierte* die Erscheinungen, so wie Locke die Verstandesbegriffe . . . insgesamt *sensifizierte* . . . hatte. Anstatt im Verstande und der Sinnlichkeit zwei ganz verschiedene Quellen von Vorstellungen zu suchen, die aber nur *in Verknüpfung* objektiv gültig von Dingen urteilen könnten, hielt sich ein jeder dieser grossen Männer nur an eine von beiden, die sich ihrer Meinung nach unmittelbar auf Dinge an sich selbst bezöge, indessen dass die andere nichts tat, als die Vorstellungen der ersteren zu verwirren oder zu ordnen.[3]

Kant himself never has a moment's doubt as to the importance, the essential character, of our 'Sinnlichkeit', which he

---

[1] W. Wundt, *Metaphysik*, in the volume on *Systematische Philosophie*, 2. durchgesehene Aufl., 1908, in *Die Kultur der Gegenwart* (Teil 1, Abtlg. 6, pp. 114–15), edited by P. Henneberg.

[2] Cf. *op. cit.*, p. 37, for Spinoza and Leibniz, p. 38 f. for the latter. 'Es ist Raum in ihm (Leibniz) für das halb Bewusste und Unbewusste—also auch Raum für Geschmack und Gefühl.' Note also the remarks on the *nescio quid* concession, so frequently made by Leibniz, and also those on 'Lust' and 'Liebe'.

[3] Kant, *op. cit.*, 2. Auf. *Transzend. Logik* (Analytik), ii. Buch (Anal. der Grundsätze), *Anmerkg. zur Amphibolie der Reflexionsbegriffe*, p. 327 (Schmidts Volksausg., pp. 120–1). Cf. *ibid.*, pp. 59 f.

does not hesitate to speak of (*op. cit.*, p. 60) as 'unsere Art der Anschauung'. It may be wise to leave Leibniz out of count, holding his views to be ambiguous. The rigorists (*die Weisen*) referred to by Hyperion must surely be earlier, not later, teachers than Leibniz, and cannot be held, with Zinkernagel, to include, much less to represent, Kant. It would be far easier to argue, at need, that it is the (one) 'wise man' of the succeeding fragments who introduces *Kantian*[1] arguments into his commentary on the Platonic myth of Eros. But this reflection brings us to our second section. The attempt must now be made to show that 'der weise Mann' (*Hyperion-*fragment in Zinkernagel's edition, vol. ii, p. 247) speaks a language very closely resembling certain utterances of Herder, to whose views Hölderlin appears to me to be making such direct reference in this fragment that one need scarcely look to Schiller, still less to Fichte, for an intermediary between Hölderlin and Plato.[2]

## II. Der Weise Mann.

The (one) wise man, whom Hyperion visited on his travels, is clearly opposed to the (many) wise men, whose doctrines

[1] See *Kritik d. reinen Vernunft*, 2nd ed., pp. 71 f. (*Von der Zeit*, iv), in which Kant attacks the prejudices of 'Natural Theology', which presupposes an object of thought, 'der ihm [dem Denker] selbst durchaus kein Gegenstand der sinnlichen Anschauung sein kann'. Here 'ist man sorgfältig darauf bedacht, von aller seiner Anschauung (denn dergleichen muss alles sein Erkenntis sein, und nicht *Denken*, welches jederzeit Schranken beweist) die Bedingungen der Zeit und des Raumes wegzuschaffen. Aber mit welchem Rechte kann man dieses tun', &c. Franz Erhardt, *Bleibendes und Vergängliches in der Philosophie Kants* (Leipzig, 1926) states the essential fact about Kant's recognition of the part played by *Empfindungen* in our thinking-process bluntly, but, I believe, quite correctly thus: 'Wenn . . . in der Marburger Schule der Versuch gemacht wird, die Empfindungen aus der Genesis unserer Erkenntnis womöglich auszuschalten, so ist das von ihrem Standpunkt aus in gewissen Sinne freilich konsequent; aber zugleich ist es völlig unkantisch und an sich ganz ungereimt, da wir von dem Wirklichen ausser unserem eigenen Selbst nur auf Grund von Empfindungen etwas wissen' (*op. cit.*, p. 89 *foot*). In this point Kant and Herder seem to me to be in essential agreement. But, if this is granted, we ought not to accept the description of the young Hyperion as having become 'a Kantian rigorist'.

[2] The pages which follow were first published in the *Modern Language Review*, vol. xxii, no. 1, January 1927.

had taught him to despise the senses and form a low opinion of Nature. It does not, however, follow that he is to be identified with any one individual wise man known to Hölderlin. The very fact that his doctrines embody not only the myth of Eros from Plato, but also a commentary on this myth, goes to prove this. Arguments have been put forward for both Schiller (recently by Claverie) and Fichte (earlier by Zinkernagel) as Hölderlin's 'model'. More probably he is a composite picture drawn from Plato, Rousseau, Schiller, Kant, Heinse, Bouterwek, and, as I shall now try to show, above all Herder, with whom one must necessarily here couple Hemsterhuis. To the latter we may devote the minimum of attention, remarking only (1) that it was he who, not only in the *Lettre de Dioclès à Diotime sur l'Athéisme* (of 1787), but also in *Alexis* and elsewhere, drew into prominence the views of this 'sage et sacrée' instructress of Socrates; (2) that he insisted, in *Alexis*, that the third and final Age of Gold would only arrive when man 'verra distinctement les bornes de son intelligence dans les faces de l'univers qu'il peut connoître'; and (3) that, while laying stress on the higher faculties possessed by 'l'être pensant', he insists upon the necessity and validity of the senses which are the medium of 'cette acquisition des idées primitives, commune à l'homme et à la brute'.[1]

More important still for us is Hemsterhuis's *Lettre sur les Désirs* (of 1770),[2] since it called forth a dissertation by Herder, the value of which, for our fragments, would seem to have

---

[1] *Lettre sur l'homme et ses rapports, Œuvres philosophiques de F. Hemsterhuis,* nouvelle éd., Paris, 1809, i, p. 138. It is worth noting that Hemsterhuis has a good deal to say on this point of the likeness and unlikeness of man and beast. At p. 139 he cites from Cicero, *De Officiis,* the following sentence: 'Inter hominem et beluam hoc maxime interest, quod haec tantum, quantum sensu movetur, ad id solum, quod adest, quodque praesens est, se accommodat, paululum admodum sentiens praeteritum aut futurum.' This is further proof, if any were necessary, that this contrast (Mensch—Tier) belongs to the *koinê* of thought in this age and also that Cicero's authority was still worth invoking.

[2] *Œuvres,* ed. cit., i, pp. 61–90, where it is immediately followed by the essay by Herder (pp. 91–130) in French, and with the title: '*De l'Amour et de l'Égoïsme,* par M. J. J. Herder.' [J. J. is a misprint for J. G.]

been overlooked. Herder called his essay *Liebe und Selbstheit* and wrote it as a commentary on Hemsterhuis's *Lettre sur les Désirs*. This was not Herder's earliest attack upon rationalism, but it may be cited here because it comes closest to Hölderlin's fragment. Before turning to it, let me quote two or three paragraphs from Herder's essay *Vom Erkennen und Empfinden, den zwo Hauptkräften der Menschlichen Seele* (1775),[1] in which he emphasizes the truth that 'Erkennen' exists 'nie ohne Empfindung' and deals faithfully with the failure of Descartes and his successors to explain the relationship of the two:

Darf ich einige Proben von den Mängeln der vorhergenannten Einseitigkeit geben? Seit *Des-Kartes* das Denken zu seinem ganzen zweifelnden Ich machte, welche Systeme sind aufkommen, Eins unnatürlicher als das Andre. Er hing die Seele in der Zirbeldrüse auf, und liess sie denken; wie nun aber den Körper bewegen? Sie kanns nicht . . . Gott musste kommen und ihn bewegen; die Denkerin auf ihrem ruhigen Teppich winkt ihrer Sklavin nur Gelegenheit zu. Also Des-Kartes. Spinosa, ein durchdringenderer Geist, der Theologe des Kartesianismus brachte beides dahin, wohin Des-Kartes Eins brachte; warum sollte der Gedanke nicht so gut unmittelbare Würkung und Eigenschaft Gottes sein, als die Bewegung? Alle Individuen erloschen also dem denkenden wie dem bewegenden Gotte. Beide sind Eigenschaften Eines Wesens, die Spinosa weiter untereinander zu bringen vergass oder verzweifelte, da er sie so weit von sich geschoben hatte. Er war ins Empyreum der Unendlichkeit so hoch hinaufgeschwindelt, dass alle Einzelnheiten ihm tief unterm Auge erblichen; dies ist sein Atheismus und wahrlich kein andrer. Leibniz kam, fürchtete den Abgrund, stand aber an Des-Kartes Ufer. Es blieb, die Seele könne den Körper nicht bewegen, Gott, in jedem Moment auch nicht: wie aber, wenn der Körper sich selbst bewegte? wenn sein Urheber dafür von Anbeginn gesorgt hätte, obs gleich kein Mensch

---

[1] *Sämtliche Werke*, ed Suphan, viii (1892), pp. 263 f. The paragraphs cited are from p. 266. Cf. also *ibid.*, pp. 169 f. and especially pp. 176 (on Liebe), 179 (on Achilles), 181 (influence of body on soul), and 185 f. (on Sinne). Finally (p. 233), Herder says roundly: 'Alles sogenannte *reine Denken* in die Gottheit hinein ist Trug und Spiel, die ärgste Schwärmerei. . . .' Cf. p. 98, line 13, below.

angeben könnte, wie? Nur dass er der Denkerin immer gerade komme—und so ward das schöne System der prästabilirten Harmonie daraus, mit seinem herrlichen Gleichniss der zwo Uhren: das witzigste System und das passendste Gleichniss, das je erdacht ward.—

Welche todte, hölzerne Uhr ist nun Seele und Seelenlehre geworden. In allen gegenseitigen Wahrnehmungen des Denkens und Empfindens entgehet ihr innige Ableitung, Fruchtbarkeit und Wahrheit.

In ihrem vielartigen, tausendfach organisirten Körper fühlt sich die Seele mit allen ihren Kräften *lebend*; selbst ihre Kraft zu erkennen und zu wollen sind nur Resultate, Aggregate dieser Verbindung: durch Aktion und Reaktion auf diesen Körper voll Empfindungen, voll Reize, ist sie nur im Universum *gegenwärtig*: selbst das Bewusstseyn von sich entgeht ihr sonst . . .

*'Selbst das Bewusstseyn von sich entgeht ihr sonst.'* How much more than this did Hölderlin need for his argument?[1] Nothing surely that is not to be found in Plato on the one hand and in Herder's later essay on *Liebe und Selbstheit* on the other.

This essay follows Herder's version of the letter of Hemsterhuis, *Sur les Désirs*, to which the translator attached a 'preliminary reminder' of the 'wealth of ideas, beauty and rarity' of this letter, in the course of which he writes:

Vielleicht hat seit Plato über die Natur des Verlangens in der menschlichen Seele niemand so reich und fein gedacht als unser Autor. Sein System ist gross wie die Welt, ewig wie Gott und unsre Seele.

But his remarks were written down hastily and contain certain obscurities of expression, due to 'die Französisch-Metaphysische Sprache, die unsrer Philosophie fremd ist'.[2] These Herder seeks to clear up in his essay.

---

[1] Even the 'Tier-Mensch-himmlisches Wesen' triad is here. Cf. Herder, *S.W.S.* *loc. cit.*, p. 268: 'Siehe eine Aufgabe, wie die menschliche Seele gross und weit und tief . . . sie wagts, den grossen Zwist ins Auge zu nehmen, nach dem der Mensch ausser und in sich Thier und Engel, Pflanze und Gott ist.

Der Engel im Menschen wie lässt er sich zum Thier herunter? die menschliche Pflanze, wie blühet in ihr Gott?'

[2] Cf. Herder's *Sämtliche Werke*, xv, p. 56, and for what follows, *ibid.*, pp. 304 f.

It begins with the 'schöne Sage der ältesten Dichtung, dass Liebe die Welt aus dem Chaos gezogen' and points out that the idea common to all versions of this story is 'dass Liebe die Wesen vereinige, wie Hass sie scheide', but it was soon discovered 'dass diese Liebe *Grenzen* habe, und eine völlige Vereinigung der Wesen in unserm Weltall selten oder gar nicht stattfinde'. This, too, was seen to be a wise ordinance of the Creator, who thus provided for the 'vesten Bestand einzelner Wesen'. The two forces, love and hate, were the counterparts of those in Nature—'*Anziehung* und *Zurückstossung*'. Herder proceeds

und ich glaube, es war schon *Empedokles*, der Hass und Liebe zu Zeichnerinnen des Umrisses aller Geschöpfe machte:[1] durch Hass, sagte er, werden die Dinge getrennt, und jedes *Einzelne* bleibt was es ist: durch Liebe werden sie verbunden und gesellen sich zu einander, sofern sie sich nehmlich ihrer Natur nach, gesellen können: denn freilich auch über die Liebe, sagten die Griechen, herrscht das *Schicksal*: und *Nothwendigkeit*, die älteste der Gottheiten, ist mächtiger, als die Liebe. Nach Platons Ideen ward diese von der *Dürftigkeit* und dem *Überfluss* in den Gärten Jupiters gebohren; sie hat also die Natur beider, und ist immer abhängig von ihren Eltern.

The doctrine of Empedocles on love and hate, modified by the doctrine of Ananke, and the two brought together by the use of the Platonic myth of the birth of Eros, we have them here in a single paragraph of Herder's, and any one who turns from this to Hölderlin's lines[2] beginning:

'Das volle Maas,' begann er nun, 'woran
Des Menschen edler Geist die Dinge misst,
Ist gränzenlos, und soll es seyn und bleiben . . .'

---

[1] Cp. *Empedocles Agrig.*, ed Sturz, Leipzig, 1805, p. 516, ll. 74–6, and pp. 566 f. Herder cites the Greek thus:

Εν δε κοτω διαμορφα και ανδιχα παντα πελονται
Συν δ' εβη εν φιλοτητι και αλληλοισι ποθειται
Εκ των γαρ παντ' οσσ' ην, οσσα τε εστι και εσται.

[2] *Sämtliche Werke*, ed. Zinkernagel, ii, p. 249.

and proceeding via the struggle with 'der ehernen Nothwendigkeit', to the concept of 'die Melodien des Schiksaals':

> Verstandst du sie? Dasselbe
> Bedeuten seine Dissonanzen auch,

thus leading up to the marriage of Poros and Penia, must surely say to himself, 'Herder here quite certainly offered Hölderlin every element he needed for this metrical fragment.'

But, lest any one still doubt, let us follow Herder further. He deals at once with the question of 'consciousness', for to Herder there is no consciousness without feeling, and says:

> Die Gottheit hat es weise und gut gemacht, dass wir unser[1] Daseyn nicht *in uns*, sondern nur durch *Reaction* gleichsam in einem Gegenstande ausser uns fühlen sollen, nach dem wir also streben, für den wir leben, in dem wir doppelt und vielfach sind.

Nature offers so many 'anziehende Gegenstände' of such varying force that our heart and life 'gleichsam eine Harmonika des Verlangens, das Kunstgebilde einer immer *reinern, unersättlichen, ewigen*[2] Sehnsucht würde'.

A little later Herder asks:[3]

> Wie kann, was Körper ist, mit dem reinen Geist Eins werden? zwo Dinge, die eigentlich nichts mit einander gemein haben, und nur durch eine Art freiwilliger Trunkenheit, wie die Griechen dichteten, ursprünglich vermischt werden konnten.

From this he proceeds to the praise of friendship as a higher, purer state than love, but only to admit that Nature saw

> dass diese reine himmlische Flamme für uns auf Erden meistens zu fein wäre [and therefore gave it] irrdische, sinnliche Reize,

---

[1] v.l. 'Unser eigen Daseyn.' Cp. Hölderlin's lines (*ibid.*, p. 253):
'Der leidensfreie reine Geist befasst
Sich mit dem Stoffe nicht, ist aber auch
Sich keines Dings und seiner nicht bewusst,
Für ihn ist keine Welt, denn ausser ihm
Ist nichts—'
'Leidensfrei' equals 'gefühlsfrei' here.
[2] Italicized words are spaced in Suphan's text.
[3] *Sämtliche Werke*, xv, p. 309.

und nun erschien Venus Urania als—Aphrodite. Liebe soll uns zur Freundschaft laden, Liebe soll selbst die innigste Freundschaft werden.[1]

Discussing the various forms of love Herder comes to the question of our enjoyment of God: 'aber wie wird der ewige genossen? durch Anschauung? oder durch Empfindung?' He sees the analogy between St. Theresa's heavenly love and the more common earthly love which may also be the cause of 'Ohnmacht' in the lover: 'denn in den Säften des Körpers ist Liebe und Liebe an Wirkungen gleich, wer auch der Gegenstand seyn möge'. The human heart must beware; 'selbst im Strom der göttlichen Liebe bleibts immer nur ein menschliches Herz . . .'

Our *isolated individual being*, Herder adds, necessitates 'die Grenzen, die unserer Liebe und Sehnsucht hienieden bei jedem Genuss gesetzt sind'. For, he points out in the following paragraph (*op. cit.*, p. 321), and here comes quite close to Hölderlin's language,[2]

Wir sind *einzelne Wesen*, und müssen es seyn, wenn wir nicht den *Grund* alles Genusses, unser eigenes *Bewusstseyn*, über dem Genuss aufgeben, und *uns selbst* verlieren wollen, um uns in einem andern Wesen, das doch nie wir selbst sind und werden können, wieder zu finden. Selbst wenn ich mich, wie es der Mysticismus will, in Gott verlöre, und ich verlöre mich in ihm, ohne weiteres Gefühl

---

[1] *Ibid.*, p. 313. I find it necessary to remark that I had written this essay up to this point before receiving the *Deutsche Vierteljahrsschrift* for July 1926 (iv, Heft 3) which contains the important essay by W. Böhm on 'Hölderlin als Verfasser des "Ältesten Systemprogramms des deutschen Idealismus" ', in which a general reference is made to the strong influence on Hölderlin of both Hemsterhuis and Herder in their anti-rationalistic writings, including Herder's *Über Liebe und Selbstheit*. Böhm, however, looks on the 'Jüngling' as a 'Kantian' rigorist *pur sang*, to whom are addressed the 'Mahnungen' of the wise man, a view which seems to me untenable so far as this rigorism is attributed to Kant.

[2] It seems worth while specially stressing the point that Herder is here opposing the ideas not of Kant, but of the mystics, teachers like Heinrich Suso (Seuse) who assert that 'so man die Kreatur erkennet in Gott, . . . so schauet man die Kreatur ohne alle Unterschiede, aller Bilden entbildet und entgleichet in dem Einen, das Gott selbst in sich selber ist' (H. Suso, hsgbn. von Wilhelm von Scholz = *Die Fruchtschale*, Bd. XIV, p. 214 [München and Leipzig, n.d.]).

und Bewusstseyn *meiner*: so genösse *Ich* nicht mehr; die Gottheit hätte mich verschlungen, und genösse statt meiner. Wie gut hat es also die Vorsehung gemacht, dass sie das Saitenspiel unsrer Empfindungen nur nach und nach, in sehr verschiednen Klängen und Arten wecket, dass sie unsre Sehnsucht jetzt auffodert, jetzt einschränkt, unser Verlangen hier thätig, dort leidend übet, über-all aber, auch nach dem süssesten Genuss, uns auf unser armes Ich zurückwirft, sagend gleichsam: 'Du bist doch ein einge-schränktes, einzelnes Geschöpf! Du dürstest nach Vollkommen-heit, aber du hast sie nicht! Verschmachte nicht am Brunnen dieses einzelnen Genusses, sondern raffe dich auf und strebe weiter.' Lasset uns dieses in einigen auffallenden Proben und Beispielen sehen.

The next paragraph interests us chiefly for its picture of the human being as tyrannically inclined.

Der Mensch ist ein Tyrann des Weltalls; aber wie bald ist auch dieser kleine Tyrann, wenn er in den Grenzen der Natur bleiben will, vom Raube gesättigt!

Hölderlin's phrase 'das alles Begehrende, alles Unterjo-chende' rises here inevitably to our memory, and we almost seem to be reading *his* words when Herder continues

Ein Tyrann, der alles allein seyn, der alles verschlingen will, wie Saturn seine Kinder, ist weder zur Freundschaft, noch zur Liebe, selbst nicht einmal zur Vaterzärtlichkeit fähig. Er drückt und unterdrückt: neben ihm kann nichts wachsen, geschweige, dass es mit ihm zusammen wachse zu Einer gemeinschaftlichen Krone.

'Auch das wird hieraus offenbar', Herder returns to this point to insist (*ibid.*, p. 323),

dass die Anziehungskraft einer einzelnen menschlichen Seele sich ins *Unendliche* weder ausbreiten könne, noch ausbreiten dörfe. Die Natur hat schmale Grenzen um jedes Einzelne gezogen; und es ist der gefährlichste Traum, sich unumschränkt zu denken, wenn man eigenschränkt ist, sich Despot des Weltalls zu glauben, wenn man von nichts als einzelnen Allmosen lebt . . .

After another digression Herder comes back once more to illustrate his thesis with a striking simile:

Unmöglich kann er [sc. der Einzelmensch] also wie Meeresschleim mit *allem* zusammenfliessen, unmöglich alles *in gleichem Grade* lieben, loben und gutheissen. . . . Er schadet damit dem Guten so sehr als dem Bösen, und verliert zuletzt ganz sein Urtheil und seinen Standpunkt. Wer nicht zurückstossen kann, kann auch nicht anziehn; Beide Kräfte sind nur *Ein Pulsschlag* der Seele.

The reference to the theory of Empedocles could not be clearer. And in the final paragraph Herder insists again, like Hölderlin, on the law of our being, the necessity of a 'Gegenstand' for our feelings, thoughts, and activities:

Um zu geben, müssen immer Gegenstände seyn, die da nehmen; um zu thun, andre, für die man thue . . . Und was endlich den Genuss des höchsten Wesens anbetrift; o da bleibts immer 'Hyperbel mit ihrer Asymptote,' wie unser Autor [sc. Hemsterhuis] [1] sagt, und muss es bleiben. Die Hyperbel nähert sich der Asymptote, aber sie erreicht sie nie: zu *unsrer* Seligkeit können wir nie den Begrif unsers Daseyns verlieren, und den unendlichen Begrif, dass wir *Gott* sind, erlangen. Wir bleiben immer Geschöpfe, wenn wir auch die Schöpfer grosser Welten würden. Wir nahen uns der Vollkommenheit, unendlich vollkommen aber werden wir nie. Das höchste Gut, was Gott allen Geschöpfen geben konnte, war und bleibt eignes Daseyn, in welchem eben Er ihnen ist und von Stuffe zu Stuffe mehr seyn wird *Alles in Allem.*

These passages from Herder's *Liebe und Selbstheit*, bearing definitely on Hemsterhuis's essay on Desire (*Verlangen*), have been cited fully because they seem to contain all that Hölderlin needed by way of encouragement to grasp the Platonic myth of Eros in his own fruitful way. The fuller, more argumentative account of the inevitable connexion in us of feeling and thought which Herder offers in his essays *Vom Erkennen und Empfinden der menschlichen Seele* may be compared with the essay on 'Selbstliebe' and would, of course, strengthen

---

[1] Cf. Hemsterhuis, *Œuvres*, i, p. 90. Herder refers to S. 108, presumably of the first edition, and Suphan adds [T. Merk, Nov. 1781, S. 121, 122].

H

in Hölderlin the view there put forward. It is unnecessary to do more than quote two paragraphs from the revised version of 1778 (*Sämtl. Werke*, viii, p. 233): they are the first two general remarks with which the essay closes:

> 1. Ist etwas in ihr [sc. dieser Abhandlung] wahr: wie fein ist die *Ehe*, die Gott zwischen *Empfinden* und *Denken* in unsrer Natur gemacht hat! Ein feines Gewebe, nur durch Wortformeln von einander zu trennen. Das oberste Geschöpf scheint mit uns Ein Loos zu haben, *empfinden* zu müssen, wenn es das Ganze nicht aus sich ruft und denket. Und welches Geschöpf kann das? Keins als unsre Philosophen, die Lehrer und Lehrlinge am hohen Baume der Weisheit.
>
> 2. Alles sogenannte *reine Denken* in die Gottheit hinein, ist Trug und Spiel, die ärgste Schwärmerei, die sich nur selbst nicht dafür erkennet. Alle unser Denken ist aus und durch Empfindungen entstanden, trägt auch, Trotz aller Destillation, davon noch reiche Spuren. Die sogenannten reinen Begriffe sind meistens reine Ziffern und Zeros von der mathematischen Tafel, und haben, platt und plump auf Naturdinge unsrer so zusammengesetzten Menschheit angewandt, auch Ziffernwerth. Dem Manne, der in der ganzen neuern Metaphysik diese Geisterchen aufsucht und abthut, dess warten mehr als des Gespensterhelden *Thomasius* Ehrenkränze; nur muss er sich auch nicht für manchem leeren Schrecken, und für Griffen dieser Geisterchen in sein Gesicht, fürchten.

To this we need add only a sentence or two from the version of 1774 (*ibid.*, viii, p. 255), in which the idea of our limitation is still more clearly brought out:

> Den edelsten, endlichen Geist können wir uns nicht ohne Sinnlichkeit gedenken; seine Sinnlichkeit ist aber auch voll Geistes: er umfasst ein Universum, das er sich aufs klärste und thätigste auflöset.
>
> Das Hauptgesetz also des Einflusses und der Abhängigkeit beider Kräfte liegt in der Natur des eingeschränkten, endlichen Wesens. Durch Empfinden lernts nehmlich erkennen: Sinne und Gefühl sind ihm der reichste, leichtste und angenehmste Ausdruck des Guten und Wahren. Es steht an einem noch unentzieferten

Weltall und lernts entziefern, die allgemeinen Eigenschaften desselben, die Göttlicher Natur sind, in seine Natur auflösen.

This argument for Herder's influence on the genesis of the metrical fragments of *Hyperion* is, I hope, full enough to convince those who can still look at this question with an open mind. Naturally I am not the first to see that Hölderlin and Herder were closely related in mind and temper. Adolf von Grolman spoke of Herder in 1919 as 'diesem Hölderlin in vielem so nah verwandten Geist' and drew attention (in *Fr. Hölderlins 'Hyperion'*, Karlsruhe, 1919, p. 8, n. 3) to Klaiber's reference to 'die seelische Ähnlichkeit Hölderlins und Herders'. The Swiss writer, Herr K. E. Hoffmann, in a review of Betzendörfer and Haering's *Neuaufgefundene Jugendarbeiten Hölderlins* (*Sonntagsblatt der Basler Nachrichten*, May 14, 1922, No. 20), which he has been so kind as to send me, drew special attention to Herder's influence on the young Hölderlin in the following words:

Zweifellos war Hölderlin schon im Stift mit *Herders* ästhetisch-kritischen Jugendschriften, besonders aber mit dem Werke Herders 'über den Geist der ebräischen Poesie,' wahrscheinlich eben durch den Stiftsephorus Schnurrer bekannt geworden; denn *Herdersche* Gedanken sind für diese schülerhafte Jugendarbeit Hölderlins bestimmend geworden.

Betzendörfer in his very useful little work on *Hölderlins Studienjahre im Tübinger Stift* (Heilbronn, 1922) brings together the names of Hemsterhuis and Herder: pointing out Hölderlin's special interest in the former, he remarks: 'Mit besonderer Vorliebe studierte er (Hölderlin) die Schriften des holländischen Philosophen Hemsterhuis, den Herder so sehr schätzte.' He reminds us that it is not improbable that Hölderlin followed Hemsterhuis's example in choosing the name of Diotima (instead of Melite) for his heroine in the final form of *Hyperion*. As is well known, Hemsterhuis gave this name to his correspondent, the Princess Amalie von Gallitzin. But the idea may have been original. Through Conz, Bardili, or

H 2

some other mentor he had already become acquainted with parts of Plato's works,[1] and it was to Plato's solution of the problems of knowledge and of the beautiful that he was being led as early as 1790. By 1792 he was acquainted with the *Republic*, for, as Betzendörfer's researches in the college library at Tübingen have shown, the only two volumes Hölderlin ever borrowed from the library were volumes vi and vii of the Zweibrücken edition (1781–7) of Plato, with the notes of Marsilius Ficinus, and these contain the *Politicus*, the *Minos*, and the *Republic*. If, as we may assume, Hölderlin at this time read the *Republic* he would thereby become familiar with the Platonic assumption of the three elements of the human psyche—reason, will, and feeling. We also see clearly from the *Parallel between Solomon and Hesiod* of 1790, as Betzendörfer has pointed out,[2] that Hölderlin's aesthetic ideas are at this period those of Mendelssohn rather than of Kant. We may, in fact, assert that the platonic and neo-platonic emphasis upon the feeling of the soul for beauty is fundamental and personal in Hölderlin.[3] For Hölderlin the poet in man precedes the philosopher, not merely historically, but psychologically, as inevitably as for Herder the child (aus dem Orient) and the 'Jüngling' (der Grieche) precede the man of ripe judgement (der Römer) and of grey-haired age and wisdom (medieval and modern man).

Fräulein Erdmann in her praiseworthy zeal to establish Hölderlin's independence of feeling and thought turns his relation to Herder almost upside down when she remarks (p. 34): 'In Herders "Ältester Urkunde des Menschengeschlechts" findet sich der Werdensgedanke sehr Hölderlinisch "in dem ewigen Wechsel von Licht und Nacht", von

---

[1] Cf. Betzendörfer, *Hölderlins Studienjahre*, pp. 30 and 128 (note 87) and my remarks in part I of my book. See also Betzendörfer, *op. cit.*, p. 46: 'Das Schöne ist nach Hölderlin [in the *Parallele* of 1790] Gegenstand des Empfindungs- und Begehrungsvermögens.'     [2] *Jugendarbeiten*, p. 18.
[3] Cf. *Sämtliche Werke*, ed. Zinkernagel, ii, 108–9 and the very pertinent remarks of Veronika Erdmann, *Hölderlins ästhetische Theorie*, Jena, 1923, pp. 9 ff.

Schlummer und Tätigkeit gesehen: dass aus der Nacht alles komme, steht auch in Hölderlins "Brod und Wein." ' It would be pertinent to remark that this idea is as old as man: the day itself is born of the night, and in the Hebrew myth of the creation, recorded so poetically in the beginning of the book of Genesis, we have it already in perfect form. It is useless and misleading to treat Hölderlin as though he were devoid of personality and originality, but equally vain to think of him as one who had neither education nor teachers. He was, as Zinkernagel rightly observed some twenty years ago, 'ganz besonders ein Kind seiner Zeit', so much so, in fact, that he stood deeply rooted in the religion, philosophy, and psychology of his age before he began *Hyperion* or approached the *Critiques* of Kant. With such a training as he had in Denkendorf, Maulbronn, and Tübingen it could not be otherwise. It should never be forgotten that the study of theology was the real aim of this education, but this included the history of philosophy, portions of the patristic works, Latin and Greek philosophy (especially the pre-Socratic), and at least an introduction to modern ideas of philosophy and psychology.[1]

We may feel sure that by 1792 Hölderlin's mind was thoroughly well prepared to accept the lead of Hemsterhuis[2] and Herder and to find in the Platonic myth of Eros a solution of the riddle of consciousness and also, in part at least, a thesis for his novel. The metrical fragments show us how this solution was reached. Their spirit and, in part, even their letter seem very largely due to Herder.

[1] Cf. Part I, ch. v of my book; Betzendörfer, *Studienjahre*, ch. ii, esp. pp. 39–44; and Erdmann, *op. cit.*, p. 47, where due stress is laid on the pre-Socratic influence. The Germans have, however, somewhat strangely hitherto failed to realize that a clear understanding of Hölderlin's theological studies in the *Stift* and their exact effect upon his views must throw fresh light on his development as a philosophical thinker. Zinkernagel has recently and properly called attention to Böhm's failure to investigate this problem in his otherwise valuable critical biography of Hölderlin. But perhaps the second volume will make good this omission.
[2] Jansen's *Collection des Œuvres philosophiques de M. F. Hemsterhuis*, the second edition of which I have cited above, was first published in 1792.

# V

## HÖLDERLIN'S IDEALS AS REFLECTED IN
## *HYPERION* AND *DER TOD DES EMPEDOKLES*[1]

I T is with some misgivings that I venture to offer my reflections on this subject. Hölderlin is a famous poet, yet not
really well known. Within the present century a great change
has come over his reputation in Germany. There is no dearth
of literature concerning him now. But there is a lack of
minute historical and critical inquiries into the development
of his mind and art, and no adequate biography of the poet
has been written[2]. Nevertheless, in Germany, among the
younger critics at least, he is now attracting almost as much
notice as his greatest contemporaries. The great events of the
last few years have been the publication of all the riper fruits
of the poet's 'Barockzeit', of several weighty critical studies,
of Hellingrath's two essays, and, in 1921, of *Die Briefe der
Diotima* (Frau Susette Gontard) by Frida Arnold, Hölderlin's
great-niece, with valuable notes by Carl Viëtor. Gradually
the mind and heart of this great German singer and seer
have been revealed to his own people and to all those who
still hold their literature dear and precious.

I make no claim to any fresh revelations in this paper, but
merely seek to re-study briefly Hölderlin's two longest works,
*Hyperion* and *Der Tod des Empedokles*, from a particular point
of view, making use, as far as possible, of certain ideas derived
from some modern psychologists. I shall assume that both
*Hyperion* and the *Empedokles*-drama have a strongly marked
'confessional' character, without impugning for a moment
their status as works of art. It is my belief that no work of
art worthy of the name can be essentially other than a
confession or self-revelation of the artist's soul. 'Artiste, on

[1] Read before the English Goethe Society in King's College, University of
London, on November 8, 1923, and here revised for publication.
[2] W. Böhm's valuable biography has now appeared. See p. 121.

donne sa propre vie à ses créations', said Anatole France in a famous book; and Professor Claparède, who has recently reminded us of this, also recalls Nietzsche's doctrine that, beneath the philosophic systems that appear to be most impersonal and objective, we find concealed the philosopher's own ideal. In the case of Hölderlin we have to do with a poet whose subjective method is obvious to the least critical inquirer.

Here, perhaps, is the best place to explain my use of the term 'Ideals' in the light of the theory which seems to explain Hölderlin's work most adequately.

*Ich, Ich-Ideale, and Es.*

The idea of the power within us that is not ourselves is familiar to all students of Goethe (e.g. in *Egmont* or *Faust*). A modern writer, G. Groddeck, in his work, *Das Buch vom Es* (1923), has gone so far as to maintain that what we call our 'ich' or 'ego' is, in fact, essentially passive; we are, to use his own expression, 'gelebt' by unknown powers we cannot control. This work is known to me only through a very interesting study by Sigmund Freud, who has taken up the idea and modified it.[1] Freud accepts Groddeck's 'Es'—a term perhaps derived from Nietzsche, to indicate the non-personal and, so to speak, 'Naturnotwendige' in our being —but attempts to delimit its powers as compared and contrasted with those of the 'ego' or 'ich'. Very roughly speaking, we may say that for him the Ich is the conscious, the Es the unconscious, of his earlier doctrine. The Ich, however, is not sharply separated from the Es: on its under side it merges in the Es. But, further, and this is important, 'das Verdrängte' is also part of the Es, through which it can communicate with the Ich. The Ich is directly influenced by the outer world, and tries to govern the Es, substituting the

[1] S. Freud, *Das Ich und das Es*, Leipzig, 1923. (There is now an English translation, in which the terms employed are the *Ego* and the *Id*. I have thought it best to leave these terms in the original German.)

'principle of reality', as far as possible, for the 'principle of pleasure', which, by nature, rules the Es. The Ich represents 'Vernunft und Besonnenheit', the Es contains the passions. The Ich, though it governs the movements in general, cannot always control the Es: like the rider of a spirited horse, it must sometimes allow itself to be carried out of the desired path.[1] So far there is nothing startling; the surprise comes with the theory, arising out of analysis of given cases, that there are persons in whom self-criticism and conscience, in themselves highly valuable, are 'unconscious', but very powerful. 'Nicht nur das Tiefste, auch das Höchste am Ich kann unbewusst sein' (Freud). Such persons have an 'unbewusstes Schuldgefühl', an idea which leads us to the analysis of the 'Über-Ich' or 'Ich-Ideal'. Freud had earlier differentiated two parts of the Ich, the second part, the Über-Ich, being less conscious than the original Ich.

This Über-Ich becomes what is normally called the conscience: it is not a mere residuum of the 'identification with the father', but has a negative side. It does not merely warn the boy to be like his father, but also not to attempt to put himself on a level with his father in certain respects. It says 'thou shalt not', as well as 'thou shalt'. The authority of other adults, religious doctrines, education, books reinforce the idea of the 'superior being' (father); the stronger the original Oedipus-complex and the speedier its repression, the more severe will the Über-Ich become later in its rule of the Ich: it may even manifest itself as an 'unconscious feeling of guilt'. Thus the psycho-analyst, long looked upon unjustly as paying no attention to the higher, more moral side of man, here gives us a reasoned account of this higher side as the Ich-Ideal, the representative of our relation to our parents. 'As little children we knew, admired, and feared these higher beings; later we absorbed them into ourselves.' It follows for

---

[1] Wilhelm Tell might supply an example. Cf. his traditional excuse:
'Wär' ich besonnen, hiess ich nicht der Tell.'

Freud that conflicts between Ich and Ideal represent essentially the opposition between the real (the outer world) and the psychical (the inner world), 'the Über-Ich being the advocate of the inner world, the Es'.

This point is made clearer in Freud's fifth chapter, to which those interested may be referred. Here it must suffice to point out that from the Ich-Ideal springs all that is highest in man, notably his religion. Important for our special subject is the conclusion that religious humility derives from the same source: the Ich compares itself with the ideal and condemns its own shortcomings. 'In the course of the child's development teachers and authorities have carried on the role of the father; their commandments, positive and negative, have remained powerful in the Ich-Ideal, and now, as conscience, exercise the moral censure. The tension between the claims of conscience and the things accomplished by the Ich is felt as a sense of guilt. The social feelings are based on identifications with other people, which are founded upon the same Ich-Ideal.' These identifications may, however, be surrogates for earlier rivalries.

Freud adds the following summary: 'From the standpoint of the limitation of the "Triebe", i.e. of morality, one can say that the Es is entirely a-moral, the Ich tries to be moral, the Über-Ich can become hyper-moral, and then it is as cruel as the Es itself. It is a remarkable fact in the human being, that the more he limits his aggressiveness towards the outer world, the more severe, that is the more aggressive, he becomes in his Ich-Ideal. The ordinary view reverses this and sees in the demands of the Ich-Ideal the motive for the suppression of the (outward) aggressiveness.' Freud, however, maintains the contrary of the common view, and asserts that the 'tendency to aggression', forbidden to seek its natural outlet, turns upon the Ich itself. 'Even the ordinary common morality of society has about it something harshly limiting, cruelly forbidding. Hence the conception of a Higher Being (νέμεσις, the Hebrew God, &c.) who punishes without mercy.'

My approach to my subject has been by way of the Freudian Ich-Ideal: others may prefer to consider the question of the evolution of a poet's ideals from a more traditional point of view. Perhaps we might find a common meeting-ground in the concept of Nemesis (with its corollary 'sense of guilt') just mentioned. That Hölderlin's mind was imbued with this sense is with me a strong conviction, and his doctrine is closely allied to that which he found in Sophocles and other Greek writers. But the origin and development of his personal attitude may be obscured by assuming too easily that he simply here takes over intellectually the Greek idea. Rather, I suggest, it lies at the root of his own Ich-Ideal, and is merely reinforced by his study of the classics and the theologians.

In the light of the psycho-analytic theory I have abandoned that of the psychiatrists, that Hölderlin's genius was unconnected with his madness, but at the same time I should deny that his 'unerreichtes Griechenideal', as such, was the cause of his mental breakdown. It so happens that his 'Griechenideale' (for he had more than one of these, and the modern may be distinguished from the ancient) are the most obvious of his ideals and have naturally attracted most attention from the essayists and biographers. They are, in fact, extremely valuable symbols of his mental life, but they belong to that part of it which is most conscious, one might almost say 'self-conscious'; they are what he chose to tell the world about. Is it not possible, even probable, that on further investigation these ideals, without turning out to be in any way valueless, may be traced to their roots in the poet's unconscious, or subconscious, mind?

The term 'unconscious' is still to some thinkers anathema: for my present purpose it will not greatly matter if any one who prefers to do so should substitute for it the term 'sub-conscious'. As to the use of the stronger term, suffice it here to recall the fact that it is no invention of the Freudian school. The germs of it are to be found in Plato: in the nineteenth century it was perhaps the French philosopher, Maine de Biran, who was first bold enough to speak of 'unconscious sensations'. His pupil, Ernest Murisier, for ten years professor of philosophy at Neuchâtel (1893–1903), in his work on *Les maladies du sentiment religieux* (1901), was a pioneer in the investigation of mental life from the pathological side, and devoted much attention to the study of the mystic ecstasy and of fanaticism. He reached the conclusion that 'the mystics sacrifice the social to the individual tendency, or "Trieb". They proceed to a unification of their personality by an elimination, which is a limitation or impoverishment of the field of conscience. They need an *idée directrice*, but, incapable of subordinating to it their other ideas, they drive them out in such a (complete) manner that it alone remains mistress of the field and reigns there with its rule (henceforth) undisputed.' It is chiefly on the hidden causes of this process, rather than on the fact, that more recent investigators have thrown light.

Returning now to Hölderlin, I shall strive to show that this poet's case, though not particularly envisaged by Murisier, might have served him for an example. Nature, however, begins her tasks quietly and proceeds step by step. So it is also with the disintegration of the mind. 'Dem Laien fallen solche Kranke überhaupt nicht als verrückt auf, wie sie ja auch noch viel später, wenn die Krankheit unver-kennbar geworden ist, vielen noch als gesund gelten': such are the words used by Professor Karl Jaspers in his book on *Strindberg und van Gogh, Versuch einer pathographischen Analyse unter vergleichender Heranziehung von Swedenborg und Hölderlin* (Bern, 1922, p. 19). It is true that Hölderlin appears to have shown no definite dementia before the year 1800, but Jaspers adds (p. 85, in dealing with Hölderlin) the double-edged statement: '(Es) bleibt eine Selbstverständlichkeit, dass der Geist nicht erkranken kann, dass er einem unendlichen Kosmos angehört, dessen Wesen unter gewissen Bedingungen nur in besonderen Gestaltungen in die Wirklichkeit tritt.' If this is true, then we have clearly to do with exactly the same 'Geist' both before and after the onset of the dementia, and may be justified in tracing back the mental struggle which ends in madness through much earlier periods, when such dementia cannot be said to exist. As Jaspers himself writes (p. 86): 'Wer aber erkennen will, fragt nach Genese und Beziehungen und lässt seinem Fragen nirgends eine Grenze setzen.' When I find Jaspers himself five pages later writing: 'In der Zeit der Krankheit geht nun allmählich —eine erschütternde Tatsache—dies bewegte und leidende Selbstbewusstsein Hölderlins in ein festes und souveränes über, indem gleichzeitig seine Dichtung sich tatsächlich nicht mehr an die wirkliche Welt wendet', and when I find him citing in close connexion herewith Hölderlin's words to Landauer in a letter written from Hauptwil in the spring of 1801, according to Christoph Schwab:

> Ich fühle es endlich, nur in ganzer Kraft ist ganze Liebe; es hat mich überrascht in Augenbliken, wo ich völlig rein und frei mich umsah. Je sicherer der Mensch in sich und je gesammelter in seinem besten Leben er ist und je leichter er sich aus untergeordneten Stimmungen in die Eigentliche wieder zurückschwingt, um so heller und umfassender muss auch sein Auge seyn, und Herz haben wird er für alles, was ihm leicht und schwer und gross und lieb ist in der Welt—

when I put these things together, I feel that I am justified in trying to trace back this 'Übergang', this 'erschütternde Tatsache', across the dividing line of 'schizophrenic symptoms', and to find in the earlier Hölderlin the kernel of the spiritual struggles, which for the later Hölderlin were resolved in this still only half-understood condition of dementia.

At least this much-tried man of thirty years is easily, almost too easily, recognized as the author of twenty-three who contributed to Schiller's *Neue Thalia* that brilliant, mystical fragment, the earliest surviving version of his *Hyperion*. It is from Hauptwil, most probably in March 1801, that was written to Landauer also the letter (No. 223) in which, full of doubt, he turns to his friend seeking the solution of his still unresolved 'Haupt-problem', that 'to be or not to be' alone, apart, unfettered, godlike, even at the price of martyrdom:

Sage mir, ist Seegen oder Fluch, diss Einsamseyn, zu dem ich durch meine Natur bestimmt und je zweckmässiger ich in jener Rücksicht, um mich selbst herauszufinden, die Lage zu wählen glaube, nur immer unwiderstehlicher zurückgedrängt bin!

Seven years earlier he had written in the end of his *Thalia*-fragment:

Abgezogenheit von allem Lebendigen, das war es, was ich suchte. Über den ehrwürdigen Produkten des altgriechischen Tiefsinns brütet' ich Tage und Nächte. Ich flüchtete mich in ihre Abgezogenheit von allem Lebendigen.

He knew then that his heart was happy in 'dieser Dämmerung'; he had even asked himself: 'Ist sie unser Element, diese Dämmerung? Warum kann ich nicht ruhen darinnen?' He had almost determined 'abzulassen von dieser verwegnen Neugier'. But the voice of his young manhood, the voice of his teachers and contemporaries had sounded in his ears with an imperative 'Thou darest not'. And so he answers himself, as one setting himself a heavy but inevitable and laudable task, 'Aber ich kann nicht! ich soll nicht (ablassen)! Es muss heraus, das grosse Geheimniss, das mir das Leben gibt oder den Tod.'

And so we see him setting out upon his fateful voyage of discovery, his search for the great secret, and we can follow him in some measure through his own utterances, his brief poignant poems, his letters to his family and friends and to the

woman he loved. But almost as readily we can follow his
evolution through his two longer and outwardly more 'objective' works, his 'novel' *Hyperion* and his fragmentary *Empedokles*-drama, if we seek carefully for the reflection of him in
these mirrors. Into these works he has projected his own
struggle to achieve the great compromise with life, to satisfy
the Über-Ich without destroying the Ich. He runs through
the gamut of experience: he turns aside from the ideal of
priest because it cannot be achieved in its purity, and tests
in spirit, one after the other, the roles of poet, lover, philosopher, soldier, tiller of the soil, hermit, shepherd of the
people. At the end he returns to the question 'Seegen oder
Fluch', and after uttering the deepest, most burning words
that he can summon to express his passion and pity and scorn
and longing and pride and sense of guilt, he follows Empedokles into the darkness, of which years ago he had asked
the unanswerable question: 'Ist sie unser Element, diese
Dämmerung?'

Let us look now for a little at the completed *Hyperion*. The
first volume was issued in 1797, the second not till 1799, the
same year in which *Empedokles* was written. Between the
two volumes there is as important a gap as between the latter
volume and the drama. The first volume and the *Thalia*-
fragment were also separated by an important period of
recasting, which cannot be discussed here.

It will be clearest for us to leave the fragments, as far as
possible, out of count and concentrate our thoughts upon the
finished volumes. We may perhaps also make certain equa-
tions, without discussing their validity: the most important
is the equation of the 'hero' Hyperion with his author, in
the sense that Hölderlin has endued his hero very largely
with his own character, thoughts, and feelings. The experiences of Hyperion are indeed imaginary, but may also be
used to throw light upon Hölderlin's ideals. And the same
may be said of the philosopher, Empedokles. If you will

allow me, I will interpret these literary works much as though they were dreams in which the dreamer is, of course, the hero and experiences either what he has himself actually experienced in his 'waking' hours or what he desires (or fears) to experience. According to our theory, we may expect to find much the same Ich-Ideal in general in both works, however the particular ideals may seem to alter. But the Ich-Ideal is itself also in process of evolution. It is accessible to influences of teachers and experience, and it seems to become more exacting as we pass from the first volume of *Hyperion* to the second, and from that to the *Empedokles*-drama.

Hyperion is a young Ionian, in love with ancient Greece and with a pure, beautiful, and wise young girl (also an Ionian)—a man with gifts of speech and vision and heart like those of a poet. But also one in violent revolt against the cold ugliness of modern life, thought, and education; one who, falling in with three teachers, is profoundly influenced in turn by each; one who, under stimulus from without and a sacred call from within, turns suddenly from being an enthusiastic orator and interpreter of the glories of the past into a soldier, and not merely a soldier but a rebel, in revolt against the constituted authority—a foreign overlordship, it is true, but the only constituted authority in the land. The poet-orator-educator throws away his lyre and girds on his sword to do battle for the faith that burns within him. He goes out, not like Saul, the son of Kish, to find his father's asses, but to find a kingdom for his oppressed fellow countrymen across the Aegean sea. But he finds nothing but cruel, selfish, barbarous brigands, void of ideals and full of sensual desires. His glorious dreams were a fool's paradise.

Had Hölderlin a 'model' for Hyperion other than himself? The question has been answered by pointing to literary works, such as Tieck's *William Lovell* and Heinse's *Ardinghello,* in which heroes of this type and various 'parallel passages' may be discovered. Recently Claverie has laid stress upon Bouterwek's *Graf Donamar* and Schiller's *Der Geisterseher* as works to which *Hyperion* is indebted. These 'sources' seem to require re-examination: perhaps, in the end, none of them is of more than secondary value. My question refers rather to the possibility of an historical character as a model for the hero; this question has not yet, I think, received adequate consideration. I am inclined to suggest, however, that some of Plutarch's heroes and one or more of the leaders in the Greek wars of rebellion of 1770, and more still of 1797–9, lent our poet such flesh and blood as he required. The facts of the war of 1770 are followed pretty faithfully, although not in any great detail. Not impossibly, the brave and warlike captain Andrutsos may have partly acted godfather to the figure of Alabanda. For Hyperion himself a nearer, in fact quite contemporary prototype, in some respects, appears in the famous poet and 'Feuergeist', Konstantinos Rhigas, 'the first martyr of Greek freedom'.[1]

Perhaps the imaginary story of Hyperion is partly founded on the historical deeds and fate of Rhigas. Hölderlin never, I think, mentions Rhigas in his correspondence or in his works: on the other hand, he followed closely the political events of his age, and, in view of his great interest in things Greek, new as well as old, one is inclined to assume that this hero's life and death must have attracted his attention. We know he 'read the newspaper' (letter to Karl Gock, August 6, 1796) and followed the 'Riesenschritte der Republikaner' in France. However this may be, the parallel between Hyperion and Rhigas seems striking enough. In each case the patriotic Greek enthusiast allowed himself to be carried away by his Es and his Ich-Ideal and paid for his want of caution by the sacrifice of his Ich. In August 1794 (Letter 94 in C.C.T.

---

[1] Cf. for Rhigas, G. F. Hertzberg, *Geschichte Griechenlands*, iii, 1878, pp. 295 ff., and on Hölderlin's keen interest in contemporary politics Zinkernagel's remark in the *Literaturblatt f. german. und roman. Philol.*, 1929, col. 254.

Litzmann's edition), Hölderlin had written to his brother
Karl words of fatherly wisdom:

Opfre nie Dein Gewissen der Klugheit auf. Aber sey klug. Es
ist ein goldner Spruch: Werft eure Perlen nicht vor die Schweine.
Und was Du thust, thue es nie in der Hitze. Ueberdenke kalt! und
führe mit Feuer aus!

The same month he wrote to Neuffer, who had lost his
'Braut': 'Welten erobern, Staaten einreissen und aufbauen
wird mir nie so gros dünken, als solchen Schmerz zu über-
winden.' Hyperion's story is for him a tale of chastening, of
ὕβρις followed by the inevitable nemesis. The hero casts his
pearls before swine. 'Der grosse Übergang aus der Jugend
in das Wesen des Mannes vom Affecte zur Vernunft, aus dem
Reiche der Fantasie ins Reiche der Wahrheit und Freiheit
scheint mir immer einer solchen langsamen Behandlung
werth zu sein', he writes (Letter 96, to Neuffer, October 10,
1794), explaining the slow growth of his story. It contains,
indeed, rightly understood, the reflexion of the death of his
own youthful false hopes and enthusiasms. The poet's way
is not the warrior's path of glory, but a way of thorns and
sorrow. The political aims, once again kindled by Fichte's
eloquence for Hölderlin, by Alabanda's mysterious charm
and inspired messages for Hyperion, are, after all, madness in one whose destiny is to lead as 'Künstler', not as
'Krieger'.

'Shakespeare ergreift Dich so ganz: das glaub' ich', Hölderlin
writes to his brother from Frankfort in March 1798 (Letter
153). 'Du möchtest auch von der Art etwas schreiben, lieber
Karl! ich möchte es auch. Es ist kein kleiner Wunsch. Du
möchtest es, weil Du auf Deine Nation mitwirken möchtest:
ich möchte es darum auch, *doch mehr noch, um in der Erzeugung
eines so grossen Kunstwerks meine nach Vollendung dürstende Seele zu
sättigen.*'

It is in the same letter that we find the pathetic cry, 'Ich suche
Ruhe, mein Bruder! . . . Bester Karl! ich suche nur Ruhe'.

But at once he pacifies the Über-Ich with the assurance that this 'Ruhesucht' is but for the moment. 'Meine seit Jahren so mannigfach, so oft erschütterte Natur will nur sich sammeln, um dann einmal wieder frisch an eine Arbeit zu gehn.' The warrior's crown is not for him, the poet's bay itself seems almost beyond his grasp: this is no 'Dichterklima', he is often 'lebensmüde'. We remember his *Schicksalslied*, learned from Adamas before he ever fell in with Alabanda. Adamas is usually and not without some reason equated with Schiller, but he may very well be, in part, a composite picture, and perhaps owes something to Conz as the representative of the doctrine of Ananke, derived largely from the Stoics. But in Schiller's *Das Ideal und das Leben* (published first as *Das Reich der Schatten* in *Die Horen*, 1795) may, I think, be clearly recognized the model for the formally so very different lines of Hölderlin, with their pregnant, unyielding contrast between the divine bliss and the blind human struggle with relentless fate, so brilliantly phrased in the last of the three verses of the *Schicksalslied*:

> Doch uns ist gegeben,
> Auf keiner Stätte zu ruhn,
> Es schwinden, es fallen
> Die leidenden Menschen
> Blindlings von einer
> Stufe zur andern,
> Wie Wasser von Klippe
> Zu Klippe geworfen,
> Jahrlang ins Ungewisse hinab.

When Hyperion sings this song of fate, Alabanda, the once envied—as perhaps Hölderlin envied Fichte—the well-beloved and loving friend ('wie Stella und sein Plato sich liebten'), the rival who refused to indulge in rivalry for the prize of Diotima's love, has just departed. And immediately upon the song follows the 'Schwanenlied' of Diotima herself, who had desired to be 'eine neue Pythia, die schlaffen Völker

mit Göttersprüchen (zu) entzünden'. In her final 'Glaubens-
bekenntnis' she prophesies to Hyperion:

Du müsstest untergehn, verzweifeln müsstest du, doch wird der
Geist dich retten. Dich wird kein Lorbeer trösten und kein
Myrthenkranz; der Olymp wird's, der lebendige, gegenwärtige,
der ewig jugendlich um alle Sinne dir blüht. Die schöne Welt ist
dein Olymp; in diesem wirst du leben, und mit den heiligen Wesen
der Welt, mit den Göttern der Natur, mit diesen wirst du freudig
seyn.

And again she cries out passionately

Die Armen die nichts kennen, als ihr dürftig Machwerk, die der
Noth nur dienen und den Genius verschmähn, und dich nicht
ehren, kindlich Leben der Natur! die mögen vor dem Tode sich
fürchten. Ihr Joch ist ihre Welt geworden; Besseres, als ihren
Knechtsdienst, kennen sie nicht; scheun die Götterfreiheit, die der
Tod uns giebt!
Ich aber nicht! ich habe mich des Stükwerks überhoben, das
die Menschenhände gemacht, ich hab' es gefühlt, das Leben der
Natur, das höher ist, denn alle Gedanken—wenn ich auch zur
Pflanze würde, wäre denn der Schade so gross?—Ich werde
seyn . . .
Trauernder Jüngling! bald, bald wirst du glüklicher seyn. Dir
ist dein Lorbeer nicht gereift und deine Myrthen verblühten,
denn Priester sollst du seyn der göttlichen Natur, und die dich-
terischen Tage keimen dir schon.
O könnt' ich dich sehn in deiner künftigen Schöne! Lebe wohl!

It would be a fascinating task to try to distinguish what
Diotima owes to Frau Gontard and what to Hölderlin himself, but this I cannot now attempt. Suffice it to say that, in
the words quoted above, the thesis of the *Empedokles-drama* is
already anticipated. The parting from Frau Gontard, whom,
it seems now certain, Hölderlin loved quite humanly with
the senses as well as with the soul, caused him to turn ever
more in upon himself in spite of her brave and loving words
in a letter of March 1799:

So lieben wie ich Dich, wird Dich nichts mehr, so lieben wie
Du mich, wirst Du nichts mehr (verzeihe mir diesen eigennützigen

Wunsch), aber verstocke Dein Herz nicht, tuhe ihm keine Gewalt, was ich nicht haben kann, darf ich nicht neidisch vernichten wollen. Denke nur ja nicht, Bester, dass ich für mich spreche. Mit mir ist das ganz anders, ich habe meine Bestimmung zum Theil erfüllt, habe genung zu tuhn in der Welt, habe durch Dich mehr bekommen als ich noch erwarten durfte. Meine Zeit war schon vorbey, aber Du solltest jetzt erst anfangen zu leben, zu handeln, zu würken, lass mich kein Hinderniss seyn, und verträume nicht Dein Leben in hoffnungslose (*sic*) Liebe.

Frau Gontard was the last, the noblest, the dearest representative of the Über-Ich for Hölderlin. His own father had died when he was an infant, his stepfather when he was a child. His dearly loved and honoured mother seemed now (cf. Briefe, No. 171) to have lost faith in him. 'O meine Mutter!' (he writes in December, 1798), 'Es ist etwas zwischen Ihnen und mir, das unsre Seelen trennt; ich weiss ihm keinen Nahmen; achtet eines von uns das andere zu wenig, oder was ist es sonst?' He comforts himself that she is afraid of spoiling her sons and so steels herself to deal with them severely. But his relation to her is essentially like that of Hyperion to his father, the child misunderstood and disowned by the best-loved parent, the first 'Träger des Über-Ichs'.

It remained for Frau Gontard by her deep love and unshaken belief in him to hold his head above the waves of doubt and draw him back from the dark waters of the 'crater' of rebirth. 'The libido', to cite Jung here, 'still has an object for the sake of which life is worth living.'[1] But even Frau Gontard is misled, or tries to mislead herself, when she writes to Hölderlin: 'Die Natur, die Dir alle edlen Kräfte, hohen Geist und tiefes Gefühl gab, hat Dich bestimmt, ein edler vortrefflicher glücklicher Mann zu werden, und es in allen Deinen Handlungen zu beweisen.' He tries hard still to fight for his place in the world of action; but in his heart of hearts he cherishes more and more 'the secret longing for the maternal depths' (Jung), and begins

[1] *The Psychology of the Unconscious*, Eng. trans., London, 1918, p. 443.

more and more clearly to express these longings, sublimated in wonderful poetic transmutation, most clearly in the *Empedokles*-drama, a work of greater depth and more pregnant force and beauty than *Hyperion*, a fitting prelude to the last wonderful lyrics.

The dramatic poem, *Der Tod des Empedokles*, concerns itself, as its title implies, with the self-destruction of the philosopher, his throwing himself, of his own volition, into the flames of Aetna. Its most complete form is that which Zinkernagel called 'die erste Fassung', and with this alone I deal.[1] It belongs to Hölderlin's Homburg period.

The legends differed as to the reasons that led Empedokles thus to take his own life. For Hölderlin Empedokles is a reflex of his own unsatisfied Ich,[2] a man conceived originally as a 'Todfeind aller einseitigen Existenz' and therefore doomed to suffering, because he cannot love and live in the 'real' world free and unfettered like a god. He is a man whose 'Sinn' is 'unbegränzt', a wonder-worker; but he has committed the unpardonable sin and likened himself to the gods themselves.

Hermokrates, the priest, says of him
> Es haben ihn die Götter sehr geliebt,
> Doch nicht ist er der Erste, den sie drauf
> Hinab in sinnenlose Nacht verstossen
> Vom Gipfel ihres gütigen Vertrauns,
> Weil er des Unterschieds zu sehr vergass
> Im übergrossen Glük, und sich allein
> Nur fühlte; so ergieng es ihm, er ist
> Mit gränzenloser Öde nun gestraft.

[1] Hölderlin later altered the character of the drama considerably.
[2] This does not preclude the possibility, to which Zinkernagel still attaches great importance, that 'Fichtes aufsehenerregender Exitus (aus Jena) vom Sommer 1795' may have influenced Hölderlin's choice of his subject. In any case the essential interest of Empedokles' fate for Hölderlin is philosophical and theological. It revives in the sharpest outline the old question of the 'Natur des eingeschränkten, endlichen Wesens' (see above, p. 98), which *ex hypothesi* cannot be 'Gott'. As Herder had put it, 'zu *unsrer Seligkeit* können wir nie den Begrif unsers Daseyns verlieren, und den unendlichen Begrif, dass wir *Gott* sind, erlangen'.

But the priest fears the end is not yet. Empedokles will awake from this strange mood of silence and despair, and in his hybris overturn

> Gesez und Kunst und Sitt' und heil'ge Sage . . .
> Wie alles sich verlor, so wird
> Er alles wieder nehmen, und den Wilden hält
> Kein Sterblicher in seinem Toben auf.

The priest succeeds in his aim, his gods smite the seer, before his great task begins. The much-feared visionary is driven out by the people of Agrigentum, who, inflamed by the priest, cry out 'Hinaus, damit sein Fluch uns nicht befleke!' Empedokles goes forth, homeless and outcast, followed only by his faithful disciple Pausanias. As he goes forth, he cries to the gods

> Ach meine Götter! im Stadium lenkt' ich den Wagen
> Einst unbekümmert auf rauchendem Rad. So möcht'
> Ich bald zu euch zurük, ist gleich die Eile gefährlich.

The second act opens in a 'Gegend am Aetna'. A peasant recognizes the outcasts, and 'der Verfluchte von Agrigent' is driven away even from this man's lowly hut. Empedokles, tasting clear water from a well, now begins to take delight in his approaching reunion with nature. Suddenly the people of Agrigentum reappear, led by Hermokrates, offering the seer pardon. In a withering storm of words he refuses to return and share their 'schauerlichen Tanz' and 'blindes Elend'. The gods have reserved for him a wholly different fate from the common death 'am seelenlosen Knechtgefühl' that is for them. So he meets and scorns them, most of all Hermokrates, and refuses the proffered crown of Agrigentum. With majestic words of warning that only by a new birth of their humanity from the ashes of all that they hold dear, from everything

> Was euch der Väter Mund erzählt, gelehrt,
> Gesez' und Bräuch', der alten Götter Nahmen,

he leaves them and passes on to his own 'Vollendung'. The

gods are mightier than we: we may deny them, but we cannot escape them. Empedokles himself had been tempted and had fallen, setting up himself and his own wisdom in the room of holy nature. This had been the cause of his strange spiritual 'Öde', described in the first act:

> Die Götter waren
> Mir dienstbar nun geworden, ich allein
> War Gott und sprachs im frechen Stolz heraus.
> O glaub'es mir, ich wäre lieber nicht
> Geboren.

But the praise of men, like their blame, has now become to him, the outcast first and then the desired leader, a mere disturbing cry. He has sought again and found the old gods: they are about to redeem their promise and fulfil the 'Sehnsucht' of his earliest infancy. He has not been 'without blemish'; he failed, as he had foreseen, to bear the glorious joys of holy nature 'taumellos', and the gods have granted his prayer that, if he failed in this, they would be willing

> Schnell ins Herz
> Ein unerwartet Schiksaal mir zu senden,
> Zum Zeichen, dass die Zeit der Läuterung,
> Gekommen sei, damit bei guter Stund'
> Ich fort zu neuer Jugend noch mich rette,
> Und unter Menschen nicht der Götterfreund
> Zum Spiel und Spott und Ärgernisse würde . . .
> Drum fordert nicht die Wiederkehr des Manns,
> Der euch geliebt, doch wie ein Fremder war
> Mit euch und nur für kurze Zeit geboren.

In the language of the psycho-analyst this is the 'return to the mother', the absolute regression of the libido, the unrestrained Narcissism, the complete withdrawal from the struggle of life. But with what richness of poetry and fullness of religious enthusiasm is it arrayed and transformed! Empedokles now longs to plunge himself in the flames of Aetna and pass through them into the divine bliss: to complete the sacrifice and the consecration in the single act of sclf-immolation. The men of Agrigentum still clamour for his presence and his aid, but he replies

> O lieber Undank! gab ich doch genug,
> Wovon ihr leben möget, I h r dürft leben,
> Solang ihr Othem habt; i c h  n i c h t. Es muss
> Bei Zeiten weg, durch wen der Geist geredet.
> Es offenbart die göttliche Natur
> Sich göttlich oft durch Menschen, so erkennt
> Das vielversuchende Geschlecht sie wieder.
> Doch hat der Sterbliche, dem sie das Herz
> Mit ihrer Wonne füllte, sie verkündet,
> O lasst sie dann zerbrechen das Gefäss,
> Damit es nicht zu anderm Brauche dien'
> Und Göttliches zum Menschenwerke werde.
> Lasst diese Glüklichen doch sterben, lasst,
> Eh sie in Eigenmacht und Tand und Schmach
> Vergehn, die Freien sich bei guter Zeit
> Den Göttern liebend opfern. Mein ist diss.
> Und wohlbewusst ist mir mein Loos und längst
> Am jugendlichen Tage hab' ich mirs
> Geweissagt: ehret mirs! und wenn ihr morgen
> Mich nimmer findet, sprecht: veralten sollt'
> Er nicht und Tage zählen, dienen nicht
> Der Sorg' [und] Krankheit, ungesehen gieng
> Er weg und keines Menschen Hand begrub ihn,
> Und keines Auge weiss von seiner Asche;
> Denn anders ziemt es nicht für ihn, vor dem
> In todesfroher Stund' am heilgen Tage
> Das Göttliche den Schleier abgeworfen—
> Den Licht und Erde liebten, dem der Geist,
> Der Geist der Welt den eignen Geist erwekte,
> In dem sie sind, zu dem ich sterbend kehre.

Never surely did any poet speak so out of his heart, yet in language so perfect and so glorious, his unquenchable longing for that here unattainable 'Götteruhe' in which

> Schicksallos, wie der schlafende
> Säugling, atmen die Himmlischen.

## BIBLIOGRAPHICAL NOTE

Full information about everything of value concerning Hölderlin down to 1922 is given in Friedrich Seebass's *Hölderlin-Bibliographie* (München, 1922). The two leading editions of the *Werke* and *Briefe* are that by von Hellingrath, Pigenot, and Seebass, complete in five volumes (Müller, München, 1915–23), and that by Franz Zinkernagel (Insel-Verlag, Leipzig, 1914–26), of which the sixth and last volume is still to appear. There are smaller editions by W. Böhm, M. Joachimi-Dege, Hans Brandenburg, and Will Vesper. The last named, published by Reclam, is perhaps the most up to date. Brandenburg's introduction to his edition (Bibliographisches Institut, Leipzig) may be had separately (*Friedrich Hölderlin, sein Leben und sein Werk*, Leipzig, 1924). The older Cotta edition, with introduction by B. Litzmann, and the *Briefe*, edited by C. C. T. Litzmann (Berlin, 1890) are still useful. W. Dilthey's essay on Hölderlin in *Das Erlebnis und die Dichtung*, though somewhat out of date, contains much that is still valuable. C. Viëtor's *Die Lyrik Hölderlins* (*Deutsche Forschungen*, Heft 3, 1921) and E. Lehmann's *Hölderlins Lyrik* (1922) are both important. W. Böhm's critical biography, *Hölderlin* (2 vols, Halle, 1928–30) recently finished, is much the fullest study hitherto attempted. Cf. my review of vol. i, in the *Modern Language Review*, vol. xxiv, 1929, pp. 100 ff., and the one by Zinkernagel in the *Literaturblatt* (cited above) for 1929, cols. 252–6. I have been unable to take account of Böhm's second volume here, but I hope to notice it shortly in the *Modern Language Review*. Lothar Kempter's *Hölderlin und die Mythologie*, Verlag der Münster-Presse, Zürich und Leipzig, 1929, is also valuable. For the early phases of Hölderlin's life and work and his relation to his predecessors the reader may be referred to my book, *Friedrich Hölderlin and the German Neo-Hellenic Movement*, Part I (Humphrey Milford, London, 1923).

PRINTED IN GREAT BRITAIN AT THE UNIVERSITY PRESS, OXFORD
BY JOHN JOHNSON, PRINTER TO THE UNIVERSITY

*BY THE SAME AUTHOR*

★

FRIEDRICH HÖLDERLIN AND
THE GERMAN NEO-HELLENIC
MOVEMENT.   PART I :  From the
Renaissance to the Thalia-Fragment
of Hölderlin's 'Hyperion' (1794).

★

*HUMPHREY MILFORD*
*OXFORD UNIVERSITY PRESS*
LONDON 1923